A SANSKRIT GRAMMAR

ALABAMA LINGUISTIC AND
PHILOLOGICAL SERIES NO. 20

A SANSKRIT GRAMMAR

BY

MANFRED MAYRHOFER

UNIVERSITY OF VIENNA

TRANSLATED FROM THE GERMAN
WITH REVISIONS
AND AN INTRODUCTION
BY

GORDON B. FORD, JR.

NORTHWESTERN UNIVERSITY

THE UNIVERSITY OF ALABAMA PRESS

Library of Congress Catalog Card Number 68–13738

ISBN 0–8173–0353–7

Printed in The United States of America

0-8173-1285-4 (pbk: alk. paper)

TRANSLATOR'S INTRODUCTION

I have translated Professor Manfred Mayrhofer's *Sanskrit-Grammatik mit sprachvergleichenden Erläuterungen*, second completely revised edition (Berlin, 1965) for the benefit of English-speaking students of Sanskrit and students of comparative Indo-European linguistics. I believe that Professor Mayrhofer's Sanskrit grammar can be used successfully in three different types of course: in elementary Sanskrit courses along with such an elementary text as Jan Gonda's *A Concise Elementary Grammar of the Sanskrit Language, with exercises, reading selections, and a glossary*, translated from the German by Gordon B. Ford, Jr. (University of Alabama Press, 1966); in courses where the linguistic structure of Sanskrit is to be presented; and, finally, in comparative Indo-European courses together with such texts as Antoine Meillet's *Introduction to the Comparative Study of the Indo-European Languages*, translated from the French by Gordon B. Ford, Jr. (University of Alabama Press forthcoming). All three groups of students should find this important book extremely useful, and I hope that its publication in an English edition will promote the study of Sanskrit in the English-speaking world.

This translation is a revised version of the 1965 German edition and incorporates suggestions made by the following reviewers: Warren Cowgill in *Language* XLI (1965), 518–20; Richard Hauschild in *Indogermanische Forschungen* LXX (1965), 215–16; F. B. J. Kuiper in the *Indo-Iranian Journal* IX (1965–6), 149–50; Wolfgang P. Schmid in the *Anzeiger für die Altertumswissenschaft* XIX (1966), 239–41; Jean-Louis Perpillou in the *Revue de Philologie, de Littérature et d'Histoire Anciennes* XL (1966), 295–6; and Hans J. Vermeer in *Kratylos* XII (1967), 207.

I am very grateful to Professor Mayrhofer for carefully reading and checking the manuscript of my translation and encouraging me in my undertaking.

GORDON B. FORD, JR.

Evanston
March 1972

CONTENTS

ABBREVIATIONS AND SYMBOLS

abl., ab. = ablative
a(cc). = accusative
act. = active
adj. = adjective
adv. = adverb
Aeol. = Aeolic
aor. = aorist
Av. = Avestan
caus. = causative
cf. = compare
comp. = comparative
d(at). = dative
du. = dual
Eng. = English
f(em). = feminine
g(en). = genitive
Ger. = German
Gmc. = Germanic
Goth. = Gothic
Gr. = Greek
Hom(er). = Homeric
IE = Indo-European
imp. = imperative
impf. = imperfect
inf. = infinitive
i(nstr). = instrumental
Lat. = Latin
lit. = literature
l(oc). = locative
m. = masculine
mid. = middle
Mid. Ind. = Middle Indic
n. = neuter
n(om). = nominative
OCS = Old Church Slavonic
OHG = Old High German
Old Ind. = Old Indic
Old Pers. = Old Persian
opt. = optative
p. = page
part. = participle
pass. = passive
perf. = perfect
p(ers). = person
pl(ur). = plural
p.p.p. = perfect passive participle
pres. = present
s. = see
s(in)g. = singular
Slav. = Slavic
subj. = subjunctive
sup. = superlative
Ved. = Vedic
v(oc). = vocative

*	=	reconstructed, unattested form
<	=	derived from
>	=	develops to, becomes
:	=	(in linguistic equations :) is related to
~	=	to be compared with
=	=	equals, is completely equivalent to

° placed with a word is used as a means of abbreviation. If, for example, for a word like *vinihatya* only the part beginning with the root is to be discussed, it is sufficient to write °*hatya* in order to avoid unnecessary repetition.

INTRODUCTION

§1. The classical form of Old Indic is called Sanskrit from Old Ind. *saṁ-skṛta-* "fitted out, correct, formed for sacred use." Sanskrit, standardized by grammarians, has remained in use as a literary and scholarly language until the present day. Classical Sanskrit developed from the Old Indic language tradition, which begins with the collection of hymns of the Rig-Veda. Passing through the stage of the later Vedic literature, poems, and theological-philosophical texts to the epic stage (§4), the language gradually reached the form that became established as "Sanskrit."[1] The distinction between Sanskrit and the older Vedic language does not lie in the domain of phonetic change but in that of morphology and vocabulary, since Sanskrit shows a loss of grammatical forms and categories as well as a loss or change in usage of a part of the vocabulary of the older language.

Concerning the latter see fundamentally L. Renou, *Journal Asiatique*, Vol. 231 (1939), pp. 321 ff.; concerning the general development of the Old Ind. language from the Rig-Veda on: J. Wackernagel–L. Renou, *Altindische Grammatik*, Vol. I² (1957), *Introduction générale*, pp. 1 ff. In this work the most important forms peculiar to the older language are in small type; cf. especially the Vedic accent (§32), special paradigms of the old language (§§50, 56), and lost categories (§85). The reader will find on p. 108 a sample of the older language.

§2. Further, this language can be traced back to earlier times, beyond the rich remains of the oldest Indic literature, by indirect evidence and with the help of linguistic methods.

a. From the middle of the second millennium B.C. remains of a language which was practically no different from Old Indic

[1] Especially outside Germany, the name *Sanskrit* is often used for Old Indic as a whole. Here, "Sanskrit" is used in the narrower sense.

are preserved in cuneiform texts of the Near East, especially from the temporarily powerful Hurrian Mitanni kingdom. Personal names which also occur in the Vedic vocabulary are found there, such as *Indaruta*, *Šubandu* = Ved. *Indrotá-*, *Subandhu-*; the names of the Old Indic gods *Indra*, *Mitra*, *Varuṇa*, and the twin gods *Nāsatyā* appear in the treaty of a Mitanni king; also, a not insignificant number of appellatives which are connected with the Hurrian element *-nni* or *-nnu* can be pointed out: *mar̯ia-nnu* "warrior using a war chariot" (= Ved. *márya-* "youth"), *mani-nnu* "necklace" (= Ved. *maṇí-* "necklace"), *babru-nnu* "brown" (= Ved. *babhrú-* "brown"), *maka-nni* "gift" (= Ved. *maghá-* "gift"), and others. Here words which we know from Old Indic are attested in texts which probably date from several centuries before the beginning of Old Indic literature; the date of that beginning certainly cannot be determined clearly. However, this similarity is only linguistic, not historical. The authors of the language remains in Asia Minor were probably offshoots of the wandering movements which led to the Indo-Europeanizing of India; however, they can have played no direct role in this Indo-Europeanization.

In addition, a recent reference, with literature: M. Mayrhofer, *Die Indo-Arier im Alten Vorderasien*, Wiesbaden, 1966.

b. Furthermore, Old Indic is so nearly related to the Iranian languages, represented in antiquity by Avestan and Old Persian, that the outlines of an "Indo-Iranian" language can still be clearly recognized, from which the languages of high culture, Old Indic and Old Iranian, proceeded as two closely connected dialects. Names of gods[2] and the designation of divine beings,[3]

[2] E.g. Old Ind. *Mitrá-* = Av. *Miθra-* name of a god; Old Ind. *Índra-* name of a god = Av. *Indra-* name of a demon; Old Ind. *Yamá-*, king of the realm of the dead, son of *Vívasvant-* = Av. *Yima-*, son of *Vivahvant-*; etc.

[3] Old Ind. *ásura-* "divine lord" = Av. *ahura-* "god, divine lord"; Old Ind. *devá-* "god" = Av. *daēva-*, Old Pers. *daiva-* "demon, idol"; Old Ind. *yajatá-* "venerable, god" = Av. *yazata-* "venerable, god."

expressions of worship,[4] and an abundance of poetic and formulaic linguistic agreements[5] are to be derived from this linguistic and cultural association of Indo-Iranian times. And, finally, Indo-Iranian belongs to the large Indo-European linguistic family. For Sanskrit is an Indo-European language; it stands in a clearly recognizable, scientifically based relationship to languages of our cultural circle, such as Latin, Greek, Germanic, and Slavic. Our grammar will at times give in small type, hence without risk of confusion with the descriptive presentation, the most obvious agreements, especially with the classical languages.

Concerning Old Iranian: H. Reichelt, *Awestisches Elementarbuch*, Heidelberg, 1909; R. G. Kent, *Old Persian, Grammar, Texts, Lexicon*, New Haven, ²1953; W. Brandenstein–M. Mayrhofer, *Handbuch des Altpersischen*, Wiesbaden, 1964; Chr. Bartholomae, *Altiranisches Wörterbuch*, Strassburg, 1904, ²Berlin, 1961; *Grundriss der iranischen Philologie*, edited by W. Geiger and E. Kuhn, 2 vols., Strassburg, 1895–1904; *Handbuch der Orientalistik* (edited by B. Spuler) I, IV, 1: *Iranistik/Linguistik*, Leiden, 1958. For the comparative treatment of Old Indic and for Indo-European see the general bibliography below, pp. 113 ff.

§3. On Indian soil the Indo-Aryan language has continued its development. Several languages, which can be called collectively Middle Indic, arose from dialects of Old Indic from the middle of the first millennium B.C. on. These are not only popular languages, extant for us especially in epigraphic records,

[4] Like Old Ind. *yajñá-* "worship of a god, sacrifice" = Av. *yasna-* "worship of a god, sacrifice"; Old Ind. *hótar-* "priest, sacrificer," *hótrā-* "sacrifice" = Av. *zaotar-*, *zaoθrā-*.

[5] Of the type of Vedic *hṛdā́ . . . mánasā*, as opposed to Av. *zərᵊdā-čā manaŋhā-čā* "according to heart and mind," Ved. *mántraṁ takṣ-* and Av. *mąθrəm taš-* "make an incantation," Ved. *víśvā dvéṣāṁsi tar-* and Av. *vīspå ṱbaēšå tar-* "overcome all enmities," Ved. *víśvebhyo yajatébhyaḥ* and Av. *vīspaēⁱbyō yazataēⁱbyō* "to all divine beings," etc.—Inherited formulas of poetic language also connect Old Indic with other old Indo-European languages: thus Ved. *máhi śrávaḥ* "great fame," *iṣirá- mánas-* "powerful mind" have their exact correspondences in the Homeric μέγα κλέϝος and ἱερὸν μένος.

as in the famous inscriptions of the emperor Aśoka, but also Middle Indic literary languages like *Pāli*, the church language of southern Buddhism, and the *Prākrit* languages, which appear in varied literary use. About the beginning of our millennium the Modern Indic stage is reached, represented today by over one hundred individual languages and dialects, the most important of which are *Hindī*, the national language of India; *Bengālī*; *Gujarātī*; *Marāṭhī*; and the Gypsy languages.

Cf. for the Middle Indic languages: J. Bloch, *Les inscriptions d'Asoka*, Paris, 1950; M. A. Mehendale, *Historical Grammar of Inscriptional Prakrits*, Poona, 1948; W. Geiger, *Pāli, Literatur und Sprache*, Strassburg, 1916; R. Pischel, *Grammatik der Prakrit-Sprachen*, Strassburg, 1900. For Modern Indic: J. Bloch, *La formation de la langue Marathe*, Paris, 1920; J. Bloch, *L'Indo-Aryen du Veda aux temps modernes*, Paris, 1934; R. L. Turner, *A Comparative Dictionary of the Indo-Aryan Languages*, London, 1966.

For any deeper study of Old Indic a familiarity with Middle Indic is indispensable, not only because works of Sanskrit literature like the dramas (§4) contain Prākrit passages; Old Indic itself is also filled with Middle Indic influences. There are many words of Middle Indic origin in Sanskrit (e.g. *bhaṭṭa-* "lord" = genuine Old Ind. *bhartar-*; *bhaṭa-* "hired soldier, servant" = genuine Old Ind. *bhṛta-* "hired, hired soldier, servant"; *naṭ-* "dance" = genuine Old Ind. *nṛt-*; etc.). We also have indirect traces of Middle Indic in so-called "hyper-Sanskritisms," wrong transpositions of Middle Indic forms into the Old Ind. literary language: cf. *masṛṇa-* "soft" for Prākrit *masiṇa-*, which comes, however, from Old Ind. *mārtsna-* "crushed finely"; *prāgbhāra-* "inclined, mountain slope" for Pāli *pabbhāra-* "inclined, mountain slope," which is to be derived from Old Ind. **prahvāra-*.

Besides Middle Indic the non-Aryan language families of India, Dravidian and Munda/Austroasiatic, have influenced Old Indic strongly, certainly in vocabulary, perhaps also in details of phonology and syntax. Thus the Old Ind. words *nīra-* "water" and *mīna-* "fish" come from the Common Dravidian words **nīr* and **mīn*, cf. Tamil *nīr* "water," *mīn* "fish"; Austroasiatic language laws, whereby a prefix (*mă-*) serves for the derivation from a basic word (**taṅg* "hand"), can be recognized from Old Ind. *mătaṅga-* "elephant"; as in *hastin-*

"elephant" (: *hasta-* "hand"), the elephant here is also characterized as the bearer of a "trunk." Cf. concerning the non-Aryan influences: M. B. Emeneau, *Linguistic Prehistory of India*, *Proceedings of the American Philosophical Society*, Vol. 98 (1954), pp. 282 ff., with lit.; T. Burrow, *The Sanskrit Language* (London, 1955), pp. 373 ff.

§4. Having developed from dialects of archaic Old Indic form after a half millennium of linguistic change, Sanskrit remained in use, undergoing the further influence of Middle and Modern Indic developments, naturally in different forms, archaic and recent, popular (as in epic) and Brahman literary, finally also in forms which are clearly based on Middle Indic, like the Sanskrit of the Buddhists and Jains.[6]

The literature in Sanskrit is of immense volume. The *Vedas*, which stand at the beginning of Old Indic literature, are, of course, composed in the older language, and only the latest parts show a form of language which is equivalent to Sanskrit in the narrower sense. Included in real Sanskrit literature are, above all, the two great epics: the gigantic *Mahābhārata*, comprising over 100,000 distichs, to which some of the most famous pieces of Old Indic poetry, such as the song of *Nala* and *Damayantī*, the legend of the flood, or the philosophical-didactic poem, the *Bhagavadgītā*, belong as independent parts; and the epic of the life of the hero Rāma, the *Rāmāyaṇa*; the metrically composed collections of legends of the *Purāṇas* stand near to the old epic poetry. More certainly established in time than the old epics, whose kernel goes back to the era before Christ, are the literary epics (*Kāvya*), which were created and performed, especially at the courts of princes, in the first centuries after Christ. Kālidāsa, probably the greatest poet of ancient India, should be mentioned here as the author of two epic poems: the *Raghuvaṁśa*, the history of Raghu's family, and the *Kumārasambhava*, the prehistory of the birth of Kumāra, i.e., the god of war Skanda.

[6] Concerning the historical destinies and individual forms of Sanskrit cf. the work of L. Renou, *Histoire de la langue Sanskrite*, Lyon–Paris, 1956.

Kālidāsa is also the most important dramatic poet of Sanskrit literature. His play *Śakuntalā*, honored by Goethe, used as the model for the *Vorspiel auf dem Theater* in *Faust*, and often translated and performed in Europe, belongs to world literature. In Old Indic drama Sanskrit alternates with various Prākrit languages (§3) according to the social status of the characters speaking.

Lyric poetry in Sanskrit also owes to Kālidāsa some of its most beautiful creations, such as the wonderful "Messenger of the Clouds" or *Meghadūta*. Amaru and Bhartṛhari, who wrote shorter strophes concerned with love and wisdom, are considered the most famous lyric poets of ancient India. Epigrammatic poems are also interspersed in the rich narrative literature. The *Pañcatantra*, a collection of fables and tales, has had an influence like that of no other work in world literature; over two hundred versions occur in more than fifty languages. Other narrative works, such as the "seventy tales of the parrot" (*Śukasaptati*) or the "twenty-five tales of the demon of death" (*Vetālapañcaviṁśatikā*), likewise show the alternation of prose and verse and the use of stories within a story, which is the technique found in the book of fables of the *Thousand and One Nights*.

Finally, Sanskrit is the language of an extensive scholarly literature, mostly composed in metrical form: law and custom, politics, historiography and medicine, astronomy and astrology, philosophy, erotism, grammar and lexicography have been treated in Sanskrit works, some of which have become famous.

M. Winternitz, *Geschichte der indischen Litteratur*, 3 vols., Leipzig, 1908–1920 (Vols. 1–2 Eng. Calcutta, 1927–1933); A. Thumb–R. Hauschild, *Handbuch des Sanskrit* 1, 1 (Heidelberg, 1958), pp. 127–68; H. v. Glasenapp, *Die Literaturen Indiens*[2], Stuttgart, 1961.

GRAMMAR

A. Phonology

§5. In the phonetically arranged order of the *devanāgarī* alphabet (§6) Sanskrit has the following sound system:

Vowels (Sonants)

a	i	u	ṛ	ḷ
ā	ī	ū	ṝ	

With regard to *ṛ*, *ṝ*, *ḷ* see §7.

Diphthongs

e	o
ai	au

e, *o*, pronounced in Sanskrit as *ē*, *ō* but not provided with signs for length in the usual transcription, are designated as "diphthongs" by the Hindus; the historically diphthongal character of these sounds (§14) was revealed to them by observations within the language (e.g. alternation in sandhi [§33] and in word formation with *-ay-*, *-av-*, or composition from *-a i-*, *-a u-*; analogy of *-i- -e- -ai-*, etc. to *-ṛ- -ar- -ār-* in "gradation" [§35]).—*ai*, *au* are by origin long diphthongs (§15), but are pronounced as normal diphthongs in Sanskrit.

Consonants

Velars	k	kh	g	gh	ṅ
Palatals	c	ch	j	jh	ñ
Cerebrals	ṭ	ṭh	ḍ	ḍh	ṇ
Dentals	t	th	d	dh	n
Labials	p	ph	b	bh	m
Semivowels		y	v		
Liquids		r	l		
Sibilants	ś	ṣ	s		
Aspirate		h			

In addition: visarga (ḥ), anusvāra (ṁ), and the rare anunāsika (m̐).

The voiceless stops (*k*, *c*, etc.), voiceless aspirates (*kh*, *ch*), and the three sibilants (*ś*, *ṣ*, *s*) are considered *voiceless* sounds; all the rest (with inclusion of the vowels, sonants, and diphthongs) are considered *voiced* sounds.

§6. The written medium in which Sanskrit texts are usually set down is the *devanāgarī*, a script which runs from left to right.

It has the following signs for vowels and diphthongs:

अ a	इ i	उ u	ऋ ṛ	ऌ ḷ	ए e	ओ o
आ ā	ई ī	ऊ ū	ॠ ṝ		ऐ ai	औ au

For the consonants we find the letters:

Velars:	क ka,	ख kha,	ग ga,	घ gha,	ङ ṅa.
Palatals:	च ca,	छ cha,	ज ja,	झ jha,	ञ ña.
Cerebrals:	ट ṭa,	ठ ṭha,	ड ḍa,	ढ ḍha,	ण ṇa.
Dentals:	त ta,	थ tha,	द da,	ध dha,	न na.
Labials:	प pa,	फ pha,	ब ba,	भ bha,	म ma.
Semivowels and Liquids:	य ya,	र ra,	ल la	व va.	
Sibilants:	श śa,		ष ṣa,		स sa.
Aspirate:	ह ha.				

The visarga *-ḥ* is expressed by a colon after the preceding letter (सः = *saḥ*); the anusvāra *ṃ* by a dot placed over the preceding letter (कं = *kaṁ*).

These signs are used for the representation of Old Indic words by means of the following system:

Signs for vowels or diphthongs which stand alone, apart from few exceptions, occur only at the beginning of a word (अ *a*-).

The consonant signs contain primary *-a-*; if they are to be provided with another vowel, this is done by means of an additional sign; i.e., original क *ka* goes to का *kā* by means of ा; similarly, कि *ki*, की *kī*, कु *ku*, कू *kū*, कृ *kṛ*, कॄ *kṝ*, कॢ *kḷ*, के *ke*, कै *kai*, को *ko*, कौ *kau*.

The lack of a vowel is expressed by ् (*virāma*): क् *k*.

Consonant groups are represented by "ligatures," i.e. by entwinings of the individual signs. Examples: त्प tpa, स्म sma, ग्ध्व gdhva, composed of *ta+pa*, *sa+ma*, *ga+dha+va*.

By combination of the basic signs with the additional signs and ligatures words of Old Indic structure can be represented quite successfully in this syllabic script. Examples: सागर *sā-ga-ra* "sea"; सुहृद् *su-hṛ-d* "friend" (=*sa* with additional sign for *-u-*, *ha* with additional sign *-ṛ-*, *da* with virāma); शब्द *śa-bda* "noise" (*bda* ligature from *ba+da*).

In our more linguistically oriented presentation Sanskrit is given not in devanāgarī but in transcription.

§7. Pronunciation:

1. Short *a* had various timbres according to the phonetic environment; its most frequent timbre was that of English *u* in *but*.

2. *ṛ*, *ṝ*, and *ḷ* are syllabic liquids, as in some Slavic languages, cf. Serbocroat. *Sȑb* "Serb," Czech *vlk* "wolf." The pronunciation of *ṛ* with an *i*-sound after it, stemming from antiquity, explains the older transcriptions (*ṛi*, *ṛî*) and the popular transcription *ri*, as in *Sanskrit* (*saṁskṛta-*, §1), *Rig-Veda* (*ṛg-*), etc.

3. *e* and *o* are long: cf. §5.

4. The voiceless and voiced aspirates (*kh*, *gh*, etc.) should be pronounced like the corresponding voiceless or voiced stops, but with an aspiration coming directly afterward.

5. The palatals (*c*, *ch*, *j*, *jh*) are usually pronounced in the West as affricates, *c* like English *ch* (*much*), *j* like English *j* (*just*); popular transcriptions of Sanskrit words like *Pantschatantra* or *Maharadscha* are based on this pronunciation. But it is not correct: the Old Indic *c*, *j* were palatal stops, not affricates.

The nasals have the articulation of the series of stops with which they are placed; thus *ṅ* is velar (cf. Ger. *Engel*), *ñ* palatal (5), *ṇ* cerebral (6).

6. The cerebrals—the name translates Old Ind. *mūrdhanya-* from *mūrdhan-* n. "head" and "upper palate"—are "retroflex"

sounds, in whose articulation the tip of the tongue is bent back toward the roof of the mouth. The pronunciation of English *t*, *d* (in *too*, *done*, etc.) comes close to them.

7. *ś* is a voiceless palatal sibilant, that is, it is spoken at the front of the hard palate; Ger. *sch* in a palatal environment, e.g., in *mischen*, has a comparable sound. *ṣ* is an *ś*-sound with retroflex (6) position of the tongue, *s* a voiceless dental *s*.

8. *h* is a voiced aspirate, *-ḥ* (visarga) a voiceless aspirate.

In the pronunciation of today's Brahmans a slight sound of the preceding vowel follows the visarga in absolute word-final position: *agniḥ* = *agnih*^{i}, *devāḥ* = *devāh*^{a}.

9. The anusvāra, before sibilants, *l*, and *h*, designates the nasalization of the vowel after which it stands; this is comparable to the nasalization of vowels in French (in *on*, *cent*, *gens*, etc.). In other environments it is usually to be regarded as an abbreviation for a full nasal (in the national script, §6): *phalaṁ bharati*, *saṁbharati* are to be spoken with [*-mbh-*].

Compare the chapters on pronunciation in the handbooks of Old Indic (p. 113), the monograph of W. S. Allen, *Phonetics in Ancient India* (London Oriental Series, Vol. 1, 1953), and S. K. Chatterji, "The Pronunciation of Sanskrit," in *Indian Linguistics*, Vol. 21 (1960), pp. 61–82.

Origin of the Old Indic Sounds

§8. The *a* of Sanskrit[7] has several origins: it corresponds to IE (= Lat. and Gr.) *a*, *e*, *o*, *m̥* (= Lat. *em*, Gr. α, Germanic *um*) and *n̥* (= Lat. *en*, Gr. α, Germanic *un*):

a = *a*: Old Ind. *ájra-* m. "field, plain" = Gr. ἀγρός "field," Lat. *ager*;

a = *e*: Old Ind. *ásti* "is" = Lat. *est*;

[7] Since no distinction exists between Sanskrit and the older language in phonology (§1), we do not hesitate to choose examples from the whole realm of Old Indic and, as is usual in comparative linguistics, to designate the positions of accents that belong only to the older language (§32).

a=*o*: Old Ind. *páti*- m. "lord" = Gr. πόσις "husband";
a=*m̥*: Old Ind. *daśa* "ten" = Gr. δέκα, Lat. *decem*, Goth. *taihun*;
a=*n̥*: Old Ind. *matí*- f. "thought" = Lat. *mens*, *mentis*, Goth. *ga-munds* "memory," cf. Gr. αὐτό-ματος.

§9. Similarly, Old Ind. *ā* is derived from IE (= Lat.-Gr.) *ā*, *ē*, *ō*, as well as from the "heavy" form of the syllabic nasal, *n̥ə̯* (= Lat. *nā*, Germanic *un*):
ā=*ā*: Old Ind. *bhrā́tar*- m. "brother" = Lat. *frāter*;
ā=*ē*: Old Ind. *rā́j*- m. "king" = Lat. *rēx*, *rēg-is*;
ā=*ō*: Old Ind. *vā́c*- f. "speech, voice" = Lat. *vōx*, *vōc-is*;
ā=*n̥ə̯*: Old Ind. *jātá*- "born" = Lat. (*g*)*nātus*, Goth. *-kunds* "descended from".

Old Ind. *ā* from *m̥ə̯* is, on the other hand, not certain. Perhaps this led rather to Old Ind. *ām*.

Old Ind. *ā* also probably comes from IE short *o* when this stood in an open syllable and was followed by *r*, *l*, *m*, or *n*. This sound law explains some important differences in the morphology of Sanskrit; in the case of the *r*- and *n*-stems *dātā́ram* (= Gr. δώτορα) as opposed to *pitáram* (= Gr. πατέρα), *áśmānam* (= Gr. ἄκμονα) as opposed to *-hán-am* (< *g^{u}*hen-m̥*), see §§52, 53, 65; or the length of the root vowel in the perfect—having spread as a type by analogy—Old Ind. *cakā́ra*, see §123. This "Brugmann's law in Kleinhans' formulation" can be held in connection with the opinion that *-o-* belonged to no open syllable if *ə̯* (§11, 1) stood after the consonant following it, as is to be expected with seṭ-roots (§37). Thus, for the verbs of the 10th class (§83) and causatives (§129) with *o*-vocalism of the root syllable, we have to establish as the original division: *māráyati* "causes to die" < **mo/rei̯-*, root **mer-* (: Old Ind. *mr̥-tá-* "dead"), but *janáyati* "begets, bears" < **ǵon/ə̯ei̯-*, root **ǵenə-* (> Old Ind. *jáni-man-*, *jani-tár-*). Cf. the lit. in Wackernagel–Debrunner, *Altind. Gramm.* I² (1957), supplement, p. 8, and Kuiper, *Lingua*, Vol. 8 (1959), pp. 436 ff.

§10. Old Ind. *ĭ* and *ŭ* come from IE *ĭ* and *ŭ*:
i=*i*: Old Ind. *-cit* "also" = Lat. *-quid* (see §18);
ī=*ī*: Old Ind. *pī́van*- "fat" = Gr. πίων;
u=*u*: Old Ind. *rudhirá*- "red" ~ Gr. ἐ-ρυθρός, Lat. *ruber*;
ū=*ū*: Old Ind. *dhūmá*- m. "smoke" = Lat. *fūmus*.
Cf. further §§11 and 13.

§11. Old Ind. *i* (sometimes also *ī*) also has another origin. If it corresponds to an *a* in the Western languages, it comes from IE "schwa" (*ə*), a vowel of indefinite timbre.

Examples for *ĭ* < *ə*:

Old Ind. *pitár-* m. "father" = Gr. πατήρ, Lat. *pater*, Eng. *father*; Old Ind. *-nī-té*, 3rd sg. mid. of the 9th class (§106) = Gr. -να-ται.

IR *ə*, firmly anchored in the system as the zero grade of original long vowels (§37), shows two additional characteristics which are forcibly required by the behavior of Old Indic and Indo-Iranian:

1. It appears also as a consonant (*ə̯*); its phonetic representation as a "laryngeal" is, of course, not certain, and the comparison of *ə*, *ə̯* with the *ḫ* of Hittite has not so far been shown conclusively by the material. Intervocalic *-ə̯-* effected hiatus:

Old Ind. *rayíḥ* (**ra-ī́s*) < **reə̯-i-s*, but gen. sg. **reə-i̯-és* > **rē-i̯-és* > Old Ind. *rāyáḥ*, below §56.

2. *-ə̯-* added directly to a stop effected the aspiration of that stop (thus *tə̯* > *th*): IE **pónt-eə-s* "path" produced Indo-Iran. **pántās*, but the gen. sg. **pn̥t-ə̯-és*, **pn̥thés*, Indo-Iran. **pathás*; this inflection is also preserved in Av. *pantå*, gen. sg. *paθō*. Old Ind. *pánthāḥ*, *patháḥ* (§66) shows understandable leveling with the carrying through of *-th-*.

Cf. further §§9, 13.

§12. To the Old Ind. *ṛ*, *ḷ* correspond in some Slavic languages syllabic liquids, which certainly have obtained this value again only secondarily; the remaining languages compared here offer groups of vowel and liquid for IE *r̥*, *l̥*, namely Gr. αρ/ρα and αλ/λα, Lat. *or*, *ol*, Gmc. *ur*, *ul*:

Old Ind. *dhṛṣṇú-* "bold" ~ Gr. θρασύς;

Old Ind. *bhṛ-* "bear," cf. Lat. *fors* "chance," Ger. *Ge-burt*;

Old Ind. *śṛ́ṅga-* n. "horn" ~ Lat. *cornu*;

Old Ind. *pṛthú-* "wide" = Gr. πλατύς;

Old Ind. *vṛ́ka-* m. "wolf" = Czech *vlk*, Goth. *wulfs*.

As with consonantal *r*, *l* (§23), IE *l̥* beside *r̥* has also merged into Old Ind. *ṛ*. Old Ind. *-ḷ-* occurs only in *kḷp-* "be fitted, arrange," whose etymological association is not quite clear.

Old Ind. *ṝ* has arisen through the imitation of quantitative relations in comparable grammatical categories. For example, the relation *agníbhiḥ* : *agnī́n* : *agnīnā́m* (§43), *śátrubhiḥ* : *śátrūn* : *śátrūṇām* (§48), etc. had as its result that from _pitṛ́bhiḥ_ "with the fathers" the acc. pl. _pitṝ́n_ and gen. pl. _pitṝṇā́m_ were formed (§53).

§13. If IE _r̥_ or _l̥_ occurred before a vowel, Old Ind. _ir_ or _ur_ developed from it:

Old Ind. _girí-_ m. "mountain" < _*g_^{u}_r̥-í-_, Av. _ga_^{i}_ri-_, cf. OCS _gora_;
Old Ind. _gurú-_ "heavy" < _*g_^{u}_r̥-ú-_, Gr. βαρύς.

"Heavy" IE _r̥ə̯, l̥ə̯_ also occurred, represented in Old Ind. by _īr, ūr_:
Old Ind. _dīrghá-_ "long" < _*dl̥ə̯-ghó-_, Av. _dar_^{ə}_γa-_, cf. Gr. δολιχός;
Old Ind. _pūrṇá-_ "full" < _*pl̥ə̯-nó-_, cf. Lat. _plēnus._

Thus, here lies a further source of Old Ind. _ī̆, ū̆_ (§10).

The rule that _-ə̯-_ disappears between vowels or sonants (§11, 1) but remains in effect before consonants is again clearly shown in this connection:

IE _*pl̥ə̯ú-_ "much" (: root _*pelə-_ > Old Ind. _párī-ṇas-_ "abundance") > Old Ind. _purú-_, with the behavior of simple preconsonantal _-l̥-_ a result of the disappearance of _-ə̯-_; but feminine _*pl̥ə̯-u̯í-_ > Old Ind. _pūrví-_, with _-ūr-_ from _-l̥ə̯-_. See also §59.

§14. The "diphthongs" _e_ and _o_, still recognizable within Indic as compounds of _a+i_, _a+u_ (§5) and probably still pronounced [_ai_], [_au_] at the beginning of the history of the Old Indic language, go back in the first place to _ai_, _au_ (Av. _aē_, _ao_, Old Pers. _ai_, _au_), which further —corresponding to the origin of _a_ from IE _a_, _e_, _o_ (§8)—come from the IE diphthongs _ai_, _ei_, _oi_ or _au_, _eu_, _ou_.

_e=ai_: Old Ind. _édha-_ m. "firewood," cf. Gr. αἴθω "inflame";
_e=ei_: Old Ind. _éti_ "goes" = Gr. εἶσι, Lat. _it_;
_e=oi_: Old Ind. _véda_ "knows" = Gr. οἶδα, Goth. _wait_;
_o=au_: Old Ind. _ójas-_ n. "strength," cf. Lat. _augustus_ "exalted";
_o=eu_: Old Ind. _śrómata-_ n. "favorable hearing," cf. OHG _hliumunt_ "reputation";
_o=ou_: Old Ind. _loká-_ m. "open space" = Old Lat. _louco-_, Lat. _lūcus_ "wood."

Old Ind. _e_ and _o_ come also from _*az_, which is sometimes of importance for the interpretation of the morphology; cf. §§30, 1; 33, 12; 60; 66; 88; 98; 124.

§15. Old Ind. _ai_, _au_ (§5) go back to the IE diphthongs with a long vowel as the first member, _āi_, _ēi_, _ōi_ or _āu_, _ēu_, _ōu_; cf. for example the dat. sg. ending of the _ā-_ and _ī_-stems, _-(āy)ai_, _-(y)ai_ (§40, 50), = Gr. (χώρ)ᾳ < _-āi_; or _gáuḥ_ m. f. "cow" = Gr. βοῦς, _*g_^{u}_ōu-s_. The fact that the second part of long diphthongs can be lost is important; cf. Old Ind. acc. sg. *gā́m* (§54), Homer. Gr. βῶν, Lat. *bō-s*, IE *$g^{u}\bar{o}(u)$-.

§16. The stops of the velar series, *k*, *kh*, *g*, *gh*, go back to two types of IE consonants: to IE velar *k*-sounds, to which *k* (Gr. κ, Lat. *c*), *g*, etc. also correspond in Lat. and Gr.; and on the other hand to the "labiovelars" like q^{u} (Lat. *qu*, Gr. π, τ, κ), g^{u}, etc. Cf.:

k=*k*: Old Ind. *kravíṣ-* n. "raw flesh" = Gr. κρέας, cf. Lat. *cruor*;

k=q^{u}: Old Ind. *ka-* interrogative pronoun (§78/2) = Lat. *quo-d*, Gr. πό-θεν, Goth. *hva-s* "who";

g[8]=*g*: Old Ind. *yugá-* n. "yoke" = Gr. ʒυγόν, Lat. *iugum*;

g=g^{u}: Old Ind. *gáti-* f. "motion" = Gr. βάσις "step," Ger. (*An-*)*kunft*;

gh=*gh*: Old Ind. *dīrghá-* "long" ~ Gr. δολιχός;

gh=$g^{u}h$ (Gr. φ, θ, χ, Lat. *f-*, *-gu-*, *-v-*, etc.): Old Ind. *gharmá-* m. "heat," cf. Lat. *formus* "warm," Gr. θερμός.

§17. Old Ind. *ṅ* is—like *ñ*—usually only a phonetic variant of the phoneme *n* in the environment of velars or palatals respectively; final *-ṅ* (in *prā́ṅ*, etc. §64) is phonemic and comes from older groups like *-*ṅk*(*s*), §33, 7.

§18. The palatals *c* and *j* go back, on the one hand, to the same IE consonants as *k* and *g*, if they stood before IE palatal vowels (*e*, *i*): IE *$q^{u}e$ "and" (Lat. *-que*) became first **ke* (§16), then **će*, Old Ind. *ca* "and." The palatalization is thus older than the change *e*>*a*, since it still presupposes *-e-*; it shows irrefutably that the Lat.-Gr. vocalic system *a*/*e*/*o* is closer to the IE original than the Old Ind. *a* (§8). Similarly *$q^{u}id$ (Lat. *-quid*) > **kid* > Old Ind. *cit* (§10); *$g^{u}\bar{i}\underset{\frown}{u}o$- "alive" (Lat. *vīvus*) > **gī̑u̯o-* > Old Ind. *jīvá-* "alive."

Old Ind. *j* goes back also to IE "palatal *ǵ*" (Lat.-Gr. *g*, but Slav. *z*, see §24), cf. *jñā-* "know" = Gr. γι-γνώ-σκω, Lat. *gnō-scō*, *nōscō*, OCS *zna-ti* "know."

The origin of Old Ind. *ch-*, word-interior *-cch-*, from IE *sḱ* is

[8] The very complex problem of the voiceless aspirates (Old Ind. *kh*, *th*, etc.) is not treated here for pedagogical reasons; beside the problematic IE voiceless aspirates cases like *tə̯* (§11, 2), Middle Indic and non-Aryan (§3), examples of expressive articulation etc. have merged into this one phenomenon. Cf. R. Hiersche, *Untersuchungen zur Frage der Tenues aspiratae im Indogermanischen* (Wiesbaden, 1964).

important, cf. Old Ind. *chāyā́-* f. "shadow" ~ Gr. σκιά; Old Ind. *gácchati* "comes," *pṛccháti* "asks," as opposed to Gr. (ἐπι-)βάσκω, or Lat. *poscō* "demand," OHG *forscōn* "seek": the present type in °*cchati* (§83) thus corresponds to the *sk*-verbs of the Western languages.

Old Ind. *jh* is rare in the older language and does not go back to Indo-European directly by means of genuine Old Indic sound laws. It was taken over in onomatopoeic words, foreign words, and words of Middle Indic origin in order to fill the empty slot in the system of stops. Concerning *ñ* see §17.

§19. Some of the cerebral stops occur in words of Middle Indic origin (like *naṭ-*, *bhaṭṭa-*, §3) and of non-Aryan origin; others have arisen legitimately in Old Ind. sound groups: thus the combination of *ṣ* or the previous stage of *ś* (§24) with *t* resulted in Old Ind. *-ṣṭ-*; the *-ta-* participles (§135) of *vṛṣ-* "rain," *dṛś-* "see" are *vṛṣ-ṭá-*, *dṛṣ-ṭá-*. Likewise in the voiced domain, IE **nizdó-* "nest" (Lat. *nīdus*, Ger. *Nest*), **mizdhó-* "price, pay" (Gr. μισθός, cf. Goth. *mizdō*) went through a stage of **niẓḍá-*, **miẓḍhá-* (with *s* [or its voiced variant *z*] to *ṣ* [*ẓ*] after *i*, §25) resulting in Old Indic *nīḍá-* "nest," *mīḍhá-* "price," with disappearance of **ẓ* and compensatory lengthening. Likewise **-źd-* to *-ẓḍ-*; see the cases in §30, 1.

§20. Old Ind. *-ṇ-* arose from original *-n-* if directly or indirectly preceded by *ṛ*, *ṝ*, *r*, or *ṣ* (except when a palatal, cerebral, or dental stood between *-n-* and the other sounds just named) and if it was followed by a vowel or *n*, *m*, *y*, *v*: thus in the case of several morphemes allomorphs with /*n*/ and /*ṇ*/ exist beside each other; cf. instr. sg. *agní-nā*, but *hári-ṇā*, *áśve-na*, but *sarpé-ṇa*, gen. pl. *áśvā-nām*, but *pitṝ-ṇām*, perf. pass. part. *lū-na-*, but *kṣī-ṇa-*.

§21. The dentals come from IE (= Lat.-Gr.) *t*, *d*, and from *dh* (= Gr. θ, Lat. *f-*, *-b-*, *-d-*); *n* is to be derived from the generally preserved IE *n*.

t = *t*: Old Ind. *tanú-* "thin," cf. Gr. τανυ-, Lat. *tenuis*;

d = *d*: Old Ind. *dáśa* "ten" = Gr. δέκα, Lat. *decem*;

dh = *dh*: Old Ind. *mádhu-* n. "sweetness, honey" = Gr. μέθυ "wine," Ger. *Met*;

n = *n*: Old Ind. *nár-* m. "man" = Gr. ἀνήρ, cf. Lat. *neriōsus*.

§22. Old Ind. *p*, *b* come from IE (=Lat.-Gr.) *p*, *b*; *bh* from IE *bh* (=Gr. φ, Lat. *f*-, -*b*-); *m* from IE *m*, which is generally preserved.

p=*p*: Old Ind. *pád*- m. "foot"=Lat. *pēs*, *ped-is*;

b=*b*: Old Ind. *bála*- n. "strength," cf. Gr. βελτίων "better," Lat. *dē-bilis* "weak";

bh=*bh*: Old Ind. *nábhas*- n. "cloud, vapor"=Gr. νέφος, cf. Lat. *nebula*;

m=*m*: Old Ind. *mātár*- f. "mother"=Gr. μήτηρ, Lat. *māter*.

§23. Old Ind. *y* and *v* continue IE *i̯* (Gr. ʽ-, ȝ-, -, Lat. *i*-, -) and *u̯* (Gr. ϝ, Lat. *v*).—Both *r* and *l* occur as continuations of IE (=Lat., Gr., Gmc.) *r* and *l*; in Old Indic, dialects which distinguished *r* and *l* have apparently merged with those which changed both liquids into *r* or both into *l*.

y=*i̯*: Old Ind. *yuván*- m. "youth" ~ Lat. *iuvenis*, Eng. *young*;

r=*r*: Old Ind. *prá*- "before, in front"=Gr. πρό, Lat. *pro*-;

r=*l*: Old Ind. *śru*- "hear," cf. Gr. κλύω;

l=*r*: Old Ind. -*lohitá*- "red" (beside *róhita*-), cf. Lat. *ruber*, Ger. *rot*;

l=*l*: Old Ind. *lubh*- "desire fervently," cf. Lat. *lubet*, Eng. *love*;

v=*u̯*: Old Ind. *náva*- "new"=Gr. νέ(ϝ)ος, Lat. *novus*.

§24. Old Ind. *ś* goes back to IE palatal *k̑*, which is continued in Latin as *c*, in Greek as κ, and in Germanic has shifted to χ (*h*); those mostly west Indo-European languages that preserve the *k*-character are called "*centum* languages." On the other hand, the "*satem* languages," to which, besides Indo-Iranian, Slavic and Baltic among others belong, change *k̑* into sibilants or spirants (Av. *s*, Old Pers. θ, Slav. *s*, Lith. *š*). Correspondingly, the voiced stop *ǵ* in the satem-domain goes to (Slav.) *z*, (Old Ind.) *j*, etc. (§18); concerning *ǵh* see §27.

ś=*k̑*: Old Ind. *śatám* "hundred"=Av. *satəm*, Old Pers. *θata*-, Lith. *šim̃tas*; Gr. ἑ-κατόν, Lat. *centum*, Goth. *hund*.

The origin of *ś* from *k̑* also becomes clear from data within Sanskrit. Thus Old Ind. *kṣ* arose from *k̑*+*s*; therefore, the *sa*-aorist of the verb *diś*- is *a-dik-ṣam* (§117). For the substantive *diś*- we find, in absolute word-final position and before endings beginning with consonants, forms like *dik*, *dig-bhiḥ* (§33, 7).

§25. Old Ind. *ṣ* has arisen from older *s*, which stood after Old Ind. *ĭ*, *ŭ*, *e*, *o*, *ṛ*, *r*, or *k*: to Gr. τέρσομαι "dry," Ger. *Durst* (**tr̥s*-) corresponds Old Ind. *tṛ́ṣ-ṇā-* f. "thirst"; to Ger. *Ochse* (**uks-*), Old Ind. *ukṣán-* m. "bull"; to the Greek superlative ending -ιστος corresponds Old Ind. *-iṣṭha-* (§72). This sound law is important for the understanding of variations in the morphology: the loc. pl. ends in *-ā-su* with the *ā*-stems, but in *-i-ṣu* with the *i*-stems, in *-ṛ-ṣu* with the *r*-stems, etc.; "you bear" is Old Ind. *bhára-si*, but "you go" is *é-ṣi*.

In the group *ṣṭ*, *ṣ* also goes back to the previous stage *ś* (§24). [See §19.]

§26. Old Ind. *s*=IE *s*; in Greek it becomes ‘- in word-initial position, disappears intervocalically, and is preserved in word-final position (-ς) and in groups (like στ, σκ); in Latin it goes to *r* between vowels, otherwise it is preserved: cf. Old Ind. *saptá* "seven"=Gr. ἑπτά, Lat. *septem*; Old Ind. *tā́sām*, gen. pl. f. of the demonstrative (§74)=Homer. Gr. τᾱ́ων, Lat. *is-tārum.*

§27. Old Ind. *h* has various origins. On the one hand, it comes from the voiced aspirates of the IE palatal series (cf. §24), *ǵh* (Gr. χ, Lat. *h*, but Slav. *z*):

Old Ind. *himá-* m. "frost, snow" (also preserved in the name of the *Himālaya* mountains)∼Gr. χειμών, Lat. *hiems*, OCS *zima* "winter."

On the other hand, it is—passing through a stage **žh*—the secondary palatalization of the previous stage of Old Ind. *gh* (IE *gh* or *g*^{u}*h*: §16); then it often stands in alternation with *gh* within the grammatical paradigm:

Old Ind. *hánti* "strikes, kills," but 3rd pl. *ghn-ánti* "they strike" (§93), *ghaná-* m. "striker, destroyer," cf. OCS *goniti* "chase, pursue."

The change of IE *dh*—which is usually preserved in Old Ind. (§21)—to *h* originates in one dialect of Old Ind.: cf. Old Ind. *hitá-* as the perfect passive participle of the root *dhā-*; *ihá* "here" (but Pāli *idha*)=Gr. ἰθαγενής "born here, of legitimate birth"; *gṛhá-* n. "house" < **gṛdhá-*, cf. Goth. *gards* "house"; sec.-ending 1st pl. mid. *-mahi* (§84)=Gr. -μεθα, etc.

In Old Ind. *gṛh-* beside *gṛbh-* "seize" and, in some further cases, *h* comes from *bh*, which again is to be ascribed to a special dialect. In Middle Indic *h* very frequently appears for *bh* and *dh*.

§28. To the visarga (*-ḥ*) corresponds final *-s* or *-r*; in sandhi the different origins are often still perceptible even without use of the comparative method (§33, 12). Cf. Old Ind. *áśvaḥ*, *agníḥ* nom. sg. = Lat. *equu-s*, *igni-s*, as opposed to *pítaḥ* voc. sg. of *pitár-*, = Gr. πάτερ.

§29. Anusvāra (*ṁ*) occurs for a nasal which happened to stand before Old Ind. *ś*, *ṣ*, *s*, or *h*: the verb of the 7th class (§102) *hi-ná-s-ti* forms as its 3rd plur. not **hi-n-s-ánti* but *hiṁsánti*; correspondingly 3rd plur. *piṁṣánti* "they trample" = Lat. *pinsunt*; *aṁhú-* "narrow" ~ Lat. *angustus*, Ger. *eng*; *áṁsa-* m. "shoulder" = Goth. *ams* "shoulder."

§30. Of combinatory sound laws only two which are of importance for the understanding of grammatical processes need be mentioned here:

1. "Bartholomae's Law of Aspirates," whereby voiced aspirates (e.g., *bh*, *dh*) + voiceless stops (e.g., *t*) go to the order voiced stops + voiced aspirates (*bdh*, *ddh*): the *ta*-participle (§135) of *labh-* "grasp" is (passing through a stage of **labh-ta-*) *labdha-*, of *budh-* "awaken" *buddhá-*. Since Old Ind. *h* goes back to *gh*, *gᵘh*, as well as to *ǵh* (> proto-Indic **źh*) (§27), various results of the meeting of Old Ind. *-h* + voiceless stop are found, depending on the previous stage of the Old Ind. sound: Old Ind. *dah-* "burn" is older **dagh-*, thus (through a stage of **dagh-tá-*) perfect passive participle *dagdhá-*, but *lih-* "lick" comes from **liźh-*, IE **liǵh-* (OCS *lizati* "lick"), thus the perfect passive participle **liźh-ta-* > **liź-dha-*, whence further **liẓḍha-*, Old Ind. *līḍha-* (§19). Since *vah-* "travel" and *sah-* "overcome" likewise go back to IE palatals, cf. proto-Indic **vaźh-* (: OCS *vez-ǫ* "I travel"), **saźh-*, the infinitives in *-tum* (§137) of these roots become *vóḍhum*, *soḍhum*, passing through a stage of **vaździhum*, **saźdhum* and **vaẓḍhum*, **saẓḍhum*; here a compensatory lengthening which changes the timbre also takes place (**az* **aẓ* > *o*, §14). In addition, see §§87, 103, 114, and 135.

2. "Grassmann's Law of the Dissimilation of Aspirates," whereby an indirect succession of two aspirates (e.g. *bh-dh*) resulted in loss of aspiration of the first sound: as the reduplicated present of *dā-* "give" is *dá-dā-ti* "gives," **dhá-dhā-ti* should have been formed from *dhā-* "put"; as a result of our sound law, however, *dádhāti* arose. Especially important is its operation in a grammatical paradigm: cf. 1st 2nd sg. mid. *dadhé*: *dhatsé* (§98) = **dha-dh-é*: **dha-dh-sé* > *dha-t-sé*, or *-dhuk* "milking," acc. sg. *-duham* < **dhugh-s* (> **dhuk-s*), acc.

**dhu(g)h-am*, where each time the first aspirate is only preserved if the second lost its aspiration by assimilation (*-dhs-*, *-ghs-* > *-ts-*, *-ks-*).

We know a similar law from Greek (without genetic connection with the Old Indic phenomenon): the reduplicated present of the root θη- was originally **thí-thē-mi* (like δί-δω-μι from the root δω-), whence by dissimilation *tí-thē-mi*, τίθημι; the declension of the word for "hair" was nom. sg. **thrikh-s* > *thrik-s* (θρίξ), but genitive singular **thrikh-ós* > *trikhós* (τριχός).

Note further the sandhi laws (§33). More thorough presentations of the history of Old Ind. phonology are offered by J. Wackernagel, *Altindische Grammatik*, Vol. I² (1957), with supplements by A. Debrunner; and by A. Thumb and R. Hauschild, *Handbuch des Sanskrit*, Vol. I, 1 (1958), pp. 218 ff.

B. Accentuation

§31. The accentuation of Sanskrit which is usual today is very similar to that of Latin: in polysyllabic words the penultimate syllable is accented if it is long by nature or by position; if the penultimate syllable is short, the antepenultimate syllable is accented; in contrast to that of Latin, the accent can also move to the fourth-to-last syllable if that is the root syllable and if the penultimate and antepenultimate syllables are short.

The following are thus stressed: *bharắmaḥ* "we bear," *bharánti* "they bear"; *bhárati* "he bears," *Rāmắyaṇa* "epic of Rāma"; *dúhitaram* acc. sg. "daughter."

Consonant groups with *y* and *v* do not make the penultimate syllable long; the accent is *dắtṛbhyaḥ* "to the donors." In the case of verbs augment, reduplication syllable, and verbal prefix receive the stress according to the rules given above only when the root syllable is short; thus in Sanskrit the imperfect of the root *yā-* "go" with a long syllable is stressed *ayắt*, the perfect *yayáu*.

§32. In the older period, from the beginning until shortly before the birth of Christ, there was a different means of accentuation, which still prevails in the early Vedic texts and is also handed down by grammarians. It involves a so-called "free" accent, i.e. one not determined by number of syllables and quantity, but occurring for each form individually, and whose position must therefore be specially marked. Old Indic inherited it from Indo-European, since countless accentual positions show agreements with Greek, with Baltic and Slavic languages, and—according to the indirect evidence of Verner's Law—with Germanic. Compare:

Ved. *dhūmáḥ* m. "smoke" = Gr. θῡμός "excitement of spirit, courage";

Ved. *nábhaḥ* n. "cloud" = Gr. νέφος "cloud," Russ. *nébo* "sky";

Ved. *duhitáram* "daughter" = Gr. θυγατέρα, Lithuanian *dùkterį* < **-tér-m̥*;

Ved. *pā́t* m. "foot," acc. sg. *pā́dam*, gen. *padáḥ* = Gr. πούς, πόδα, ποδός;

Ved. *pitár-* m. "father," *bhrā́tar-* m. "brother" = Gr. πατήρ, φρᾱ́τηρ, Goth. *fadar*, *brōþar* from proto-Germanic **faþḗr*, but **ƀrṓþēr*.

C. Sandhi

§33. A striking characteristic of Sanskrit practice is that something which indeed occurs in other languages, but is usually eliminated in their written representation, is expressed in a strict system of rules: the mutual influence of final sounds and initial sounds of words following one another in the flow of speech. Our sample (§34) makes it evident that, without knowledge of these rules of "euphonic" combination—the Indians and, following them, the scientific grammar of the West, call this *sandhi-* (*saṁ-dhi-*) m. "union, combination"—the simplest Sanskrit text could not be interpreted.

The sandhi rules are:

1. Contiguous vowels of like quality (short or long) merge into the corresponding long vowel: *nāstīha* stands for separated *na asti iha* "is not here"; *jayābharat* for *jayā abharat* "the woman bore"; *yadīcchet* for *yadi icchet* "if he could wish."

2. *a*, *ā* + *i*, *ī* becomes *e*; *a*, *ā* + *u*, *ū* becomes *o*; *a*, *ā* + *ṛ* becomes

ar: *vinerṣyayā* for *vinā īrṣyayā* "without jealousy"; *sovāca* for *sā uvāca* "she spoke"; *yatharṣiḥ* for *yathā ṛṣiḥ* "like a seer."

3. *a, ā* + *e, ai* becomes *ai*; *a, ā* + *o, au* becomes *au*: *adyaiva* for *adya eva* "still today"; *tasyauṣadham* for *tasya auṣadham* "his medicine."

4. Final *i, ī, u, ū, ṛ, ṝ* change to the corresponding semivowels or liquids respectively (*y, v, r*) before unlike initial vowels: *trīṇy etāni* for *trīṇi etāni* "these three"; *astv etat* for *astu etat* "this should be"; *kartr asti* for *kartṛ asti* "it is effective."

5. Final *-e, -o* remain before short *a-*, which is eliminated: *te 'pi* for *te api* "even these"; *prabho 'tra* for *prabho atra* "you powerful one here."

Before all other vowels final *-e, -o* become *-a*: *nagara iha* for *nagare iha* "in the city here"; *prabha ihi* for *prabho ihi* "you powerful one, come."

In addition, the decomposition into *-av* (*-ay*) occurs (rarely) for *-o*, still more rarely for *-e* before any vowel but *a-*: *prabhav ihi*.

6. *-ai* becomes *-ā* before vowels; *-au* becomes *-āv*, more rarely *-ā*: *devyā iha* for *devyai iha* "to the goddess here"; *tāv ubhau* for *tau ubhau* "these two."

The final vowels *-ī, -ū,* and *-e* in forms of the dual and in *amī* "those" (§77) undergo no sandhi changes; *a-* is not elided after them, either. The same holds for short interjections. Cf. *girī iha* "the two mountains here," *i Indra* "Hey, Indra!"

7. Final original consonant groups are reduced in Sanskrit to one consonant: *bharan* nom. sg. "bearing" for **bharant-s* (: stem *bharant-*, cf. acc. *bharant-am*, + nom. ending *-s*).

In absolute word-final position only the voiceless stops (*-k, -ṭ, -t, -p*) of the velars, cerebrals, dentals, and labials (§5) can stand; other stem-final sounds are changed into voiceless stops (cf. *upaniṣad-*, acc. sg. *upaniṣad-am*, but nom. sg. *upaniṣat*). For word-final palatals and *-ś-*, *-k* appears in absolute word-final position, for *-j-* and *-ś-* sometimes also *-ṭ*: *vāc-* f., gen. sg. *vāc-aḥ* "voice" forms the nom. sg. *vāk*, *diś-* f. "point of the compass" the nom. sg. *dik*, but *viś-* f. "place" the nom. sg. *viṭ*. For *-ṣ-* and *-h-* we find *-k* and *-ṭ* in absolute word-final position. Cf. the examples of declension in §59.

These "changes" naturally have historical causes. Thus *vāk* with *-k* (from **vāk*+*s*, Lat. *vōx*) is the original form, as opposed to *vāc-aḥ*, with the palatalization of the older velar before an IE palatal vowel (: Lat. *vōc-is*) according to §18; the form *vāc-* appearing in the majority of cases is considered, nevertheless, as the "stem." In the case of *diś-*: *dik*, *-k* results from the development in word-final position of the IE *k̍* (§24) which otherwise went to *-ś-*; the change of IE palatals to *-ṭ* stems from another historical period; cf. most recently, F. B. J. Kuiper, *Indo-Iranian Journal*, Vol. 10 (1967–68), pp. 103 ff.

8. The voiceless stop in absolute word-final position (see §7) remains in sandhi only before voiceless sounds (§5); before voiced stops (*g*, *d*, etc.), voiced aspirates (*gh*, *dh*, etc.), *r*, *l*, *y*, *v*, and the vowels it becomes a voiced stop; before nasals it becomes the nasal of its class: *āsīd rājā* for *āsīt rājā* "there was a king," *abharad annam* for *abharat annam* "he brought food," or *tan mama* for *tat mama* "this of mine," *vāṅ me* for *vāk me* "my speech."

Before *h-* a voiceless stop in absolute word-final position becomes a voiced stop; *h-* then becomes the corresponding voiced aspirate: *tad dhi* for *tat hi* "for this"; *vāg ghi* for *vāk hi* "for this speech."

9. A dental is assimilated to the following palatal, cerebral, and *l*: *tac ca* for *tat ca* "and this"; *taj jalam* for *tat jalam* "this water"; *prākarṣal lavaṇāmbhasi* for *prākarṣat lavaṇāmbhasi* "he dragged over the salt sea."

Final dental + initial *ś-* gives *-cch-*: *tacchrutvā* for *tat śrutvā* "having heard this."

10. *-n* before voiced palatals (*j*, *jh*), cerebrals, and *ś-* becomes

the corresponding nasal (*ñ*, *ṇ*, *ñ*), and *ś*- can then become *ch*-: *tāñ janān* for *tān janān* "these people"; *tāṇ ḍambarān* for *tān ḍambarān* "this noise"; *tāñ śaśān* or *tāñ chaśān* for *tān śaśān* "these hares."

-*n* before *l*- becomes *m̐l*: *tām̐l lokān* for *tān lokān* "these worlds."

The anunāsika usually serves for the expression of nasalization in this group, more rarely the anusvāra (§5).

All nasals (except -*m*) that stand in word-final position after a short vowel are doubled before an initial vowel: *āsann atra* for *āsan atra* "they were here."

Between final -*n* and initial voiceless palatals (*c*, *ch*), cerebrals (*ṭ*, *ṭh*), and dentals (*t*, *th*) the corresponding sibilant (*ś*, *ṣ*, *s*) is inserted, and -*n* becomes anusvāra (*ṁ*): *vṛkāṁ-ś-ca* stands for *vṛkān ca* "and the wolves," *tāṁ-ṣ-ṭaṅkān* for *tān ṭaṅkān* "these hoes," *devāṁ-s-tatra* for *devān tatra* "the gods here" (all acc. pl.).

Considered historically, this is no "insertion"; the old group, reduced to one consonant in absolute word-final position (according to §33, 7), has been maintained in sandhi. This is comparable to the preservation of Latin final sounds in the *liaison* of French: *est-il*, Lat. *est*. *vṛkān*, *devān* go back to **vṛkāns*, **devāns*, cf. Goth. *wulfans*, Old Prussian *deiwans*, Lat. *deōs* < **deiuons*. The rule then, of course, also holds for cases in which *-*ns* was never present: *abharan* (< **abhara-nt*, cf. Lat. *laudaba-nt*) + *tatra* "they carried there" becomes *abharaṁ-s-tatra* in sandhi.

11. -*m* becomes anusvāra (-*ṁ*) before consonants: *pūrvaṁ sattvam* for *pūrvam sattvam* "the former existence."

12. The visarga -*ḥ* derives from older -*s* or -*r* (§28). -*ḥ* stands only in absolute word-final position before the voiceless stops and voiceless aspirates of the velar and labial series and before sibilants: *punaḥ punaḥ* "again and again," *puruṣaḥ khanati* "the man digs." Under all other conditions we find the final sound

changed, and we must proceed not from *-ḥ*, but from its previous stage *-s* or *-r*, to understand the results of sandhi.

(*a*) *-s*, but also *-r*, changes to *-ś* before *c-*, *ch-*, to *-ṣ* before *ṭ-*, *ṭh-*, to *-s* before *t-*, *th-*; or, more correctly, old *-s* (> *-ḥ*) remains *-s* before voiceless dental stops.

Cf. *bhrātaras trayaḥ* "three brothers"; *punaś carati* "again he wanders": *bhrātaraḥ* < *-as*, *punaḥ* < *-ar*.

(*b*) *-s*, after vowels other than *-a-* and *-ā-* becomes *-r* before voiced sounds (§5); *-r* remains *-r* under these conditions, also after *-a-*, *-ā-*: *agnir dahati* for *agnis dahati* "a fire is burning"; *naur vahati* for *naus vahati* "the ship is travelling"; *pitar atra* "you father here" (with old *-ar*, from the *r*-stem *pitar-*); *punar atra* "again there" (*-ar*).

Old *-r* or *-r*, having arisen from *-s* according to the preceding rule, disappears before initial *r-* with compensatory lengthening of a preceding short vowel: *śiśū roditi* "the child is crying" stands (through a stage of **śiśur roditi*) for *śiśus roditi*; *punā ramate* "again he enjoys himself" for *punar ramate*.

(*c*) *-as* becomes *-o* (through a stage of **-az*, §14) before voiced consonants and before *a-*; *a-* is then elided, as it is after old *-o* (§33, 5): *devo 'pi* for *devas api* "even the god"; *Nalo nāma* for *Nalas nāma* "Nala by name." Before other vowels *-as* becomes *-a*; the hiatus remains: *āditya iva* for *ādityas iva* "like the sun"; *nṛpa uvāca* for *nṛpas uvāca* "the king spoke."

(*d*) *-ās* becomes *-ā* before all voiced sounds: *nṛpā jayanti* for *nṛpās jayanti* "the kings triumph."

In word-interior position the same rules as in sentence sandhi are often to be observed: the plural instrumentals in *-bhiḥ*, for example, behave according to the rules which we know from §33, 8 and 12; for *marut-* "wind" we find *marud-bhiḥ*; for *manas-* "mind," *mano-bhiḥ*; for *cakṣus-* "eye," *cakṣur-bhiḥ*.

In addition, the discussion of the phonological history (§§8 ff.) is above all to be referred to for an understanding of sound changes in word-interior position, for example, with the contact of stem and ending: the fact that *e*, *o* go back to **ăi*, **ău* (§14) and thus appear before vowels as *ay*, *av*, or the change of *n* to *ṇ* (§20), of *s* to *ṣ* (§25).

§34. For the practical explanation of the sandhi rules (§33) we give below the first verses of a Sanskrit text, the song of Nala and Damayantī (§4), in the original; after it follows the same text, but the words appear in the form which they would have in absolute word-final position. After each form which deviates in the original as a result of a sandhi rule the number of the section of §33 in which the rule in question is explained is inserted in parentheses.

1. Original (Nalopākhyāna I 1–3):

Bṛhadaśva uvāca:

āsīdrājā nalo nāma vīrasenasuto balī
upapanno guṇairiṣṭai rūpavānaśvakovidaḥ /1/
atiṣṭhanmanujendrāṇāṁ mūrdhni devapatiryathā
uparyupari sarveṣāmāditya iva tejasā /2/
brahmaṇyo vedavicchūro niṣadheṣu mahīpatiḥ
akṣapriyaḥ satyavādī mahānakṣauhiṇīpatiḥ /3/[9]

2. Decomposition into forms in absolute word-final position:

Bṛhadaśvaḥ (12*c*) *uvāca:*

āsīt (8) *rājā nalaḥ* (12*c*) *nāma vīrasenasutaḥ* (12*c*) *balī*
upapannaḥ (12*c*) *guṇaiḥ* (12*b*) *iṣṭaiḥ* (12*b*) *rūpavān aśva-kovidaḥ* /1/
atiṣṭhat (8) *manujendrāṇām* (11) *mūrdhni devapatiḥ* (12*b*) *yathā*
upari (4) *upari sarveṣām ādityaḥ* (12*c*) *iva tejasā* /2/

[9] "Bṛhadaśva said:
'There was once a king named Nala, mighty son of Vīrasena; he was endowed with desirable virtues, of handsome form, and familiar with horses. [1]
He stood at the head of the princes of men, just as the king of the gods (stands at the head of the gods),
far, far surpassing all in splendor, like the sun. [2]
The hero, friendly to Brahmans, knowledgeable in the Veda, was prince in the land of the Niṣadhas;
he was fond of dice, spoke truthfully, and was a great leader of armies' [3]."

brahmaṇyaḥ (12*c*) *vedavit* (9) *śūraḥ* (9, 12*c*) *niṣadheṣu mahīpatiḥ akṣapriyaḥ satyavādī mahān akṣauhiṇīpatiḥ* /3/.

Cf., besides the treatments of sandhi in the handbooks (p. 113): M. B. Emeneau, *Sanskrit Sandhi and Exercises*, 2nd ed. Berkeley, 1958; W. S. Allen, *Sandhi, The Theoretic, Phonetic, and Historical Bases of Word-Junction in Sanskrit*, The Hague, 1962.

D. Gradation

§35. The qualitative and quantitative change in forms etymologically belonging to the root form, which can be gathered from examples like Old Ind. *bhṛ-ta-* "borne" (*-ṛ-*), *bhar-ati* "he bears" (*-ar-*), and *bhār-a-* m. "burden" (*-ār-*), was reduced by the Indian grammarians to a system of three grades: according to this system a fundamental grade (like *-ṛ-*) can be raised to the guna-grade (approximately, "excellence, [high] degree") by simple "gradation," i.e. an increase by short *-a-* (*-a-r-*); by a further gradation, which means an increase by long *-ā-*, vṛddhi ("increase, growth") is reached (*-ā-r-*). Since the Indians, furthermore, made the historically correct observation that *e* and *o* go back to older **a-i*, **a-u* (§§5, 14) and that *ai*, *au* are compounded from *ā+i*, *ā+u* (§15), they could set up the following system of gradation:

Fundamental grade	*ĭ*	*ŭ*	*r̥̆*	*l̥*
Guṇa	*e*	*o*	*ar* (*ra*)	*al* (*la*)
Vṛddhi	*ai*	*au*	*ār* (*rā*)	(*āl*)

Examples: fundamental grade *nī-* "lead" (p.p.p. *nī-ta-* "led"), guṇa *ne-* (*ne-tar-* m. "leader"; *nay-a-ti* "leads," §83), vṛddhi *nai-* (aorist *a-nai-ṣīt*);

Fundamental grade *śru-* "hear" (p.p.p. *śru-ta-* "heard"), guṇa *śro-* (infinitive *śro-tum*), vṛddhi *śrau-* (aorist *a-śrau-ṣīt*; caus. *śrāv-ayati* with **-āu̯-* < **-āu-*);

Fundamental grade *kḷp-* "prepare, join" (p.p.p. *kḷp-ta-* "prepared, ready"), guṇa *kalp-* (*kalp-ate* "is fitted").

§36. The basic phenomena of Indo-European ablaut are already included in this system of gradation; modern linguistics differs from Indian theory only in so far as it begins with a primary "full grade" (e.g. Old Ind. *-ar-*), from which a "zero grade" (Old Ind. *-ṛ-*) is to be derived by weakening conditioned by accent and a "lengthened grade" (Old Ind. *-ār-*) by lengthening.[10]

The Hindus, however, built the other forms on the weakest root form by means of "increment." Thereby, of course, they ruined for themselves the possibility of satisfactorily adding to the system roots with *-a-*vocalism, like *pat-* "fall"; here *ă* is considered both as fundamental grade and guṇa, *ā* as vṛddhi, whereas the real fundamental grade of the guṇa-grade *pat* (*pat-ati* "falls") and the vṛddhi *pāt* (causative *pāt-ayati*) would have to be sought in *pt* (aorist *a-pa-pt-at*).

§37. An additional recognition of IE ablaut theory was anticipated by the Indians. It is connected with the established fact that the zero grade of a primary long vowel (e.g. *ē*) is *ə* (originally *eə*:*ə* like *er*: *r̥*, §11), and concerns the IE "disyllabic bases," e.g. the theoretical base **ĝen-ē-* "beget, bear," to which the normal grades **ĝn-ḗ-* (Old Ind. *jñā-tí-* m. "relative") and **ĝen-ə-* (Old Ind. *jáni-man-* n. "birth") and the zero grade **ĝn̥-ə̥-* (Old Ind. *jā-tá-* "born," §9) belong and which is clearly to be distinguished from a root like **men-* "think" (normal grade; Old Ind. *mán-man-* n. "thought, mind"), zero grade **mn̥-* (> Old Ind. *ma-tí-* f., §8). The Indians already saw this distinction and recognized its characteristic in the presence of *-i-* (< *-ə-*, §11) in the first type (*ján-i-man*, *jan-i-tár-*, *ján-i-toḥ*, etc.). In the formal language of Old Indic grammar roots like *man-* (*ma-tí-*, *ma-tá-*, *mán-tu-*, *mán-tra-*) are called aniṭ-roots (*an-i-ṭ*, from *an-* "un-, non-": thus "without *i*"). Roots like *jan*(*ⁱ*)- are called seṭ-roots (< **sa-i-ṭ* [*-e-* < *-a* + *i-*, §§5, 14], from *sa-* "with, together": "with *i*"). Cf. further §§9, 83 (p. 71), 115, 135, 136, 137.

[10] An example of IE ablaut in the modern interpretation: the normal grade of the Gr. suffix -τερ- occurs in (πα)τέρ(α) "father" (acc. sg.), zero grade in (πα)τρ(ός) "of the father," lengthened grade in (πα)τήρ "father" (nom. sg.).

E. Morphology

1. The Noun (Substantive and Adjective)

§38. Like the classical languages, Sanskrit possesses a large number of vocalic and consonantal stems and thus has several "declensions." It has three genders: masculine, feminine, neuter; three numbers: singular, dual (as expression of the dual number), plural; eight cases: nominative, vocative, accusative, instrumental, dative, ablative, genitive, locative.

The Sanskrit nominative, genitive, dative, accusative, and vocative resemble in their use the corresponding cases in the classical languages. At any rate, the following should be emphasized: the use of the nominative before *iti* "so," in order to introduce a name (*vadanty Aparṇeti. . .tām* "she is named Aparṇā," literally "they call her [acc. *tām*]: Aparṇā; she is so [*iti*] named"); the function of the genitive sometimes approaches that of the dative: *hitaṁ tasya* "good for him."—The instrumental designates means, instrument, cause, accompaniment: *tā laguḍena tāḍayiṣyāmi* "I shall strike these with the club"; *nirayo yas tvayā vina* "Hell is what is without you." Passive constructions with the instr. are popular: *tena. . .śarāva ekaḥ prāptaḥ* "by him a pot (was) obtained" (=he obtained. . .). The ablative designates the point of departure: *lobhāt krodhaḥ prabhavati* "anger arises from avidity." The locative is the local case: *āsīt. . . nagare. . .brāhmaṇaḥ* "there was a Brahman in the city." Important is the locative absolute, comparable to the corresponding ablative or genitive constructions in Latin and Greek, respectively: *vayasi prāpte* "with attained age" (when they had become adult); *mūle hate hataṁ sarvam* "if the root (*mūla-*) is killed, everything is dead."

1. *a*-declension (m. n.)

§39. Paradigm *deva-* m. "god."

	Singular	Dual	Plural
Nom.	devaḥ	devau	devāḥ
Voc.	deva	devau	devāḥ
Acc.	devam	devau	devān

	Singular	Dual	Plural
Instr.	devena	devābhyām	devaiḥ
Dat.	devāya	devābhyām	devebhyaḥ
Abl.	devāt	devābhyām	devebhyaḥ
Gen.	devasya	devayoḥ	devānām
Loc.	deve	devayoḥ	deveṣu

Neuter: *yuga-* "yoke."

N. A.	yugam	yuge	yugāni
V.	yuga	yuge	yugāni

The remaining cases as in the masc.

Additional forms in the older (Vedic) language: sing. instr. *-ā*; dual nom.-acc.-voc. *-ā* (long vowel beside original long diphthong *-au*: §15); plur. nom. *-āsaḥ*, instr. *-ebhiḥ*, gen. *-ām.*—Neuter: plur. nom.-acc.-voc. *-ā*.

The Lat. and Gr. *o*-stems correspond historically (Old Ind. *ă* < IE **ŏ*, §§8, 9): cf. masc. sing. Old Ind. *dev-aḥ* = Gr. ἵππ-ος, Lat. *equ-os*, *-us*; Old Ind. *-a* = Gr. -ε, Lat. *-e*; Old Ind. *-am* = Gr. -ον, Lat. *-um*; Old Ind. *-asya* = Homer. Gr. -οιο; *-e* = Gr. οἴκ-οι "at home"; dual Old Ind. *-au* and (Ved.) *-ā* = Gr. ἵππ-ω, Lat. *amb-o*; plur. Old Ind. *-āḥ* = Goth. *wulf-ōs*; Old Ind. *-ān*, in sandhi *-āṁ-s°* (§33, 10) ~ dial. Gr. -ονς, Goth. *wulf-ans*. Neuter sing. *yug-am* = Gr. ʒυγ-όν, Lat. *iug-um*; plur. (Ved.) *yug-ā* = Lat. *iug-a*; etc.

2. *ā*-declension (f.)

§40. Paradigm *senā-* f. "army."

	Singular	Dual	Plural
Nom.	senā	sene	senāḥ
Voc.	sene	sene	senāḥ
Acc.	senām	sene	senāḥ
Instr.	senayā	senābhyām	senābhiḥ
Dat.	senāyai	senābhyām	senābhyaḥ
Abl.	senāyāḥ	senābhyām	senābhyaḥ
Gen.	senāyāḥ	senayoḥ	senānām
Loc.	senāyām	senayoḥ	senāsu

For *ambā-* f. "mother" the irregular voc. sg. *amba* also occurs.

Additional forms of the older language: sing. instr. *-ā*; plur. nom. *-āsaḥ*.

The *ā*-stems of the classical languages correspond historically: cf. sing. Old Ind. *sen-ā* = Gr. χώρ-ᾱ, Lat. *mens-a*, Goth. *gib-a*; Old Ind. *-ām* = Gr. -ᾱν, Lat. *-am*; plur. nom.-acc. Old Ind. *-āḥ* = Goth. *gib-ōs*.—The *-ai* of the dat. sg., the *-āḥ* of the gen.-abl. sg. are also to be compared with certainty to Gr. -ᾳ (§15), Lat. *-ae*, Goth. *-ai* or Gr. -ᾱς, Lat. *famili-ās*, *viās*, Goth. *-ōs*, respectively; for an explanation of the *-āy-* before them cf. most recently G. Liebert, *Studia Linguistica*, Vol. 14 (1960), pp. 95 ff., with lit.

§41. Adjectives of three genders arise through the joining of the masculine and neuter *-a*-declension and the feminine *-ā*-declension (§§39, 40): e.g. *pāpaḥ* m., *pāpā* f., *pāpam* n. "bad."

As Gr. νέος, νέα, νέον, Lat. *novus*, *nova*, *novum* show, this adjective type is an IE inheritance.

In addition, many adjectives have a feminine in *-ī*, cf. §50.

§42. The root nouns in °*ā*- of the type *soma-pā-* "drinking soma" are usually added here, but their endings are those of the consonant stems (§57), with which *-pā-* appears only before endings with an initial consonant (like *-m*, *-bhiḥ*), whereas *-p-* appears before endings with an initial vowel (like *-aḥ*, *-i*). We thus decline: sing. n. v. *somapāḥ*, a. *-pām*, i. *-pā*, d. *-pe*, ab. g. *-paḥ*, l. *-pi*; dual n. v. a. *somapau*, i. d. ab. *-pābhyām*, g. l. *-poḥ*; plur. n. v. *somapāḥ*, a. *-paḥ*, i. *-pābhiḥ*, d. ab. *-pābhyaḥ*, g. *-pām*, l. *-pāsu*.—This archaic type (see Wackernagel–Debrunner, *Altind. Grammat.*, Vol. III, pp. 125 ff.) is often replaced in the later language by the more frequent stems in *a-* (f. *ā-*).

3. *i*-declension

(*a*) Masculines

§43. Paradigm *agni-* m. "fire."

	Singular	Dual	Plural
Nom.	agniḥ	agnī	agnayaḥ
Voc.	agne	agnī	agnayaḥ
Acc.	agnim	agnī	agnīn

	Singular	Dual	Plural
Instr.	agninā	agnibhyām	agnibhiḥ
Dat.	agnaye	agnibhyām	agnibhyaḥ
Abl.	agneḥ	agnibhyām	agnibhyaḥ
Gen.	agneḥ	agnyoḥ	agnīnām
Loc.	agnau	agnyoḥ	agniṣu

Additional forms of the older language: sing. instr. *-yā*; gen. *-yaḥ*; loc. *-ā* (beside *-au*, cf. §39 note); plur. nom. *-yaḥ*.

Cf. the IE *-ei-*/*-i*-stems: sing. Old Ind. *agn-iḥ* = Gr. ὄφ-ις, Lat. *ign-is*; Old Ind. *-im* = Gr. -ιν, Lat. *sit-im*; plur. Old Ind. *-ayaḥ* = Gr. -εις, Lat. *-ēs*, Goth. *gast-eis* "guests"; Old Ind. *-īn*, in sandhi *-īṁ-s°* (§33, 10) ~ Goth. *gast-ins*; Old Ind. *-ibhyaḥ* ~ Lat. *-ibus*.

§44. The following are inflected irregularly:

1. *sakhi-* m. "friend" in the cases sing. nom. *sakhā*, acc. *sakhāyam*, instr. *sakhyā*, dat. *sakhye*, abl. gen. *sakhyuḥ*, loc. *sakhyau*; dual n. v. a. *sakhāyau*; plur. nom. voc. *sakhāyaḥ*.

2. *pati-* m. "lord" in sing. instr. *patyā*, dat. *patye*, abl. gen. *patyuḥ*, loc. *patyau*.—As the final member of compounds (like *gṛha-pati-* "master of the house"), and sometimes also when standing alone, it follows §43.

(*b*) Feminines

§45. Paradigm *mati-* f. "understanding."

	Singular	Dual	Plural
Nom.	matiḥ	matī	matayaḥ
Voc.	mate	matī	matayaḥ
Acc.	matim	matī	matīḥ
Instr.	matyā	matibhyām	matibhiḥ
Dat.	matyai, mataye	matibhyām	matibhyaḥ
Abl.	matyāḥ, mateḥ	matibhyām	matibhyaḥ
Gen.	matyāḥ, mateḥ	matyoḥ	matīnām
Loc.	matyām, matau	matyoḥ	matiṣu

Additional forms of the older language: sing. instr. *-ī*, loc. *-ā* (like §43); plur. nom.-acc. *-yaḥ*.

The independence of the feminine *i*-declension—originally probably no different from the *i*-masculines (§43)—is explained (1) by the preservation of archaic forms, like sing. instr. *-yā* (m. only in Ved., §43 note); (2) by analogical formations (like plur. acc. *-īḥ* beside masculine *-īn* [§43] according to the model f. *-āḥ* [§40]: m. *-ān* [§39]; (3) by an influence of the *ī*-declension [§50], to which especially the double forms like sing. dat. *-yai* (beside *-aye*), abl.-gen. *-yāḥ* (beside *-eḥ*) are due.

(*c*) Neuters

§46. Paradigm *vāri-* n. "water."

	Singular	Dual	Plural
Nom.	vāri	vāriṇī	vārīṇi
Voc.	vāri	vāriṇī	vārīṇi
Acc.	vāri	vāriṇī	vārīṇi
Instr.	vāriṇā	vāribhyām	vāribhiḥ
Dat.	vāriṇe	vāribhyām	vāribhyaḥ
Abl.	vāriṇaḥ	vāribhyām	vāribhyaḥ
Gen.	vāriṇaḥ	vāriṇoḥ	vārīṇām
Loc.	vāriṇi	vāriṇoḥ	vāriṣu

The historical basis is the IE neuter type with *i*-stem, cf. Lat. *mar-e* (from **mar-i*) n. "sea"; this was originally no different from §43 in its inflection, except in the nom.-acc. The difference is caused by the fact that the *i*-neuters (and similarly those in *-u-*, §48) have been completely influenced by the *n*-stems (§65), so that, for all cases with an initial vowel in the endings (like *-aḥ*, *-i*, *-oḥ*), we must proceed from a "stem" *vāri-ṇ-* (*-ṇ-* according to §20).

§47. The neuters *akṣi-* "eye," *asthi-* "bone," *dadhi-* "sour milk," and *sakthi-* "thigh" form the instr., dat., abl., gen., loc. sing., the gen.-loc. dual, and the gen. plur. from stems in *-an-* (thus according to §65): thus, ***asthnā***, ***asthne***, ***asthnaḥ***, ***asth*(*a*)*ni***; ***asthnoḥ***; ***asthnām***.

4. *u*-declension (m. f. n.)

The *u*-stems in Sanskrit are declined quite similarly to the *i*-stems (§§43–46), but *-u-* is to be substituted for *-i-*, *-av-* for *-ay-*, *-v-* for *-y-*, *-o-* for *-e-* (with exception of the loc. sing.).

§48. Paradigms *śatru-* m. "enemy," *dhenu-* f. "cow," *madhu-* n. "honey."

Singular

	m.	f.	n.
Nom.	śatruḥ	dhenuḥ	madhu
Voc.	śatro	dheno	madhu
Acc.	śatrum	dhenum	madhu
Instr.	śatruṇā[11]	dhenvā	madhunā
Dat.	śatrave	dhenvai, dhenave	madhune
Abl.	śatroḥ	dhenvāḥ, dhenoḥ	madhunaḥ
Gen.	śatroḥ	dhenvāḥ, dhenoḥ	madhunaḥ
Loc.	śatrau	dhenvām, dhenau	madhuni

Dual

	m.	f.	n.
N. V. A.	śatrū	dhenū	madhunī
I. D. Ab.	śatrubhyām	dhenubhyām	madhubhyām
G. L.	śatrvoḥ	dhenvoḥ	madhunoḥ

Plural

	m.	f.	n.
N. V.	śatravaḥ	dhenavaḥ	madhūni
Acc.	śatrūn	dhenūḥ	madhūni
Instr.	śatrubhiḥ	dhenubhiḥ	madhubhiḥ
D. Ab.	śatrubhyaḥ	dhenubhyaḥ	madhubhyaḥ
Gen.	śatrūṇām	dhenūnām	madhūnām
Loc.	śatruṣu	dhenuṣu	madhuṣu

Noteworthy additional forms of the older language are: masc. sing. instr. *-vā*, dat. *-ve*, abl.-gen. *-vaḥ*, loc. *-avi*; plur. nom. acc. *-vaḥ* (also f.). In the case of the neuters the stem extended by *-n-* (cf. §46) spreads only in the course of the history of the Old Indic language.

[11] *-ṇ-* from *-n-* according to §20.

Compare the (*eu-*)/*u*-declension of the related languages: Old Ind. *śatr-uḥ* = Gr. πῆχ-υς, Lat. *frūct-us*, Goth. *sun-us*, OCS *syn-ъ* "son"; Old Ind. *-um* = Gr. -υν, Lat. *-um*, Goth. *-u*; Old Ind. *-ave* = Lat. *-uī*, OCS *syn-ovi*; Old Ind. *-oḥ* = Lat. *-ūs*, Goth. *-aus*, OCS *-u*; plur. *-avaḥ* = Gr. -εες, -εις, Lat. *-ūs*, Goth. *-jus*, OCS *-ove*; *-ūn*, *-ūṁ-s°* (§§33, 10; 39; 43) ~ Goth. *-uns*; *-ubhyaḥ* ~ Lat. *-ubus*; etc.

§49. Adjectives in *-i-* are inflected like the substantives of the three genders: *śuciḥ* m. "pure" (according to §43), *śuciḥ* f. (according to §45), *śuci* n. (according to §46); but the neuter adjectives, with exception of the nom.-voc.-acc., can also be declined according to §43. A similar situation holds for the *-u*-adjectives: *tanuḥ* m. "thin" is inflected like *śatruḥ* (§48), *tanu* n. like *madhu*, but it can also follow the masculines except in the nom.-voc.-acc. More frequent than *tanuḥ* f. (like *dhenuḥ*, §48) is the feminine formation of the *u*-adjectives in *-v-ī*, thus f. *tanvī-*, which is declined according to §50.

Inherited from the common language are both the type of adjective in *-i-* (cf. Lat. *fortis*, *-e*) and that in *-u-*, as well as the peculiarity that the feminine is extended by the *-ī*/*i̯ā*-stem: cf. Old Ind. *svādú-* "sweet," f. *svādvī́* with the Gr. ἡδύς, ἡδεῖα (**su̯ādeu̯-i̯ā-*), Lat. *suāv-i-s*.

5. *ī-* and *ū*-stems (f.)

(*a*) Polysyllabic

§50. Paradigms *devī-* f. "goddess," *śvaśrū-* f. "mother-in-law."

	Singular		Plural	
Nom.	devī	śvaśrūḥ	devyaḥ	śvaśrvaḥ
Voc.	devi	śvaśru	devyaḥ	śvaśrvaḥ
Acc.	devīm	śvaśrūm	devīḥ	śvaśrūḥ
Instr.	devyā	śvaśrvā	devībhiḥ	śvaśrūbhiḥ
Dat.	devyai	śvaśrvai	devībhyaḥ	śvaśrūbhyaḥ
Abl.	devyāḥ	śvaśrvāḥ	devībhyaḥ	śvaśrūbhyaḥ

	Singular		Plural	
Gen.	devyāḥ	śvaśrvāḥ	devīnām	śvaśrūṇām[12]
Loc.	devyām	śvaśrvām	devīṣu	śvaśrūṣu

	Dual	
N. V. A.	devyau	śvaśrvau
I. D. Ab.	devībhyām	śvaśrūbhyām
G. L.	devyoḥ	śvaśrvoḥ

Exception: *lakṣmī-* f. "(goddess of) luck" forms the nom. sg. *lakṣmīḥ*. Additional nominatives in *-īḥ* also occur sporadically in Sanskrit.

The feminine of many *-a*-adjectives (§41) is formed not in *-ā* but in *-ī* and is declined like *devī-*: *sundaraḥ*, *sundarī*, *sundaram* "beautiful." The feminine of most *u*-adjectives (§49) is also formed with *-vī-*.

In the Vedic language we find two declension types in *-ī-*, clearly distinct from each other:

1. The *devī́*-inflection, with which the previously given paradigm from classical Sanskrit largely agrees. The essential deviations are dual nom. acc. *devī́* (voc. *dévī*), plur. nom. *devī́ḥ* (voc. *dévīḥ*). This type derives from stems in *-i̯ā-* which originally agreed in many respects with the old *-ā*-declension (§40) but in some cases—e.g. in the nom. sing.—carried through the ablaut grade *-ī-*. The situation continued by Old Ind. is found preserved in Gothic, among other languages: cf. Ved. *dev-ī́*, gen. *dev-yā́ḥ*, dat. *dev-yái* with Goth. *band-i* "chain," gen. *band-jōs*, dat. *band-jai*; the classical languages show indirect continuations; Lat. e.g. shows extension by means of a *-k*-suffix (Lat. *genetrīx*, *genetrī-c-is*: Old Ind. *jánitrī-* "mother"); Greek continues this tradition mostly by means of -ια-stems (πότνια: Old Ind. *pátnī*, *pátnyā-* "mistress").

2. The *vr̥kī́*-inflection (example Ved. *vr̥kī́-* f. "she-wolf"); here a primary *-ī-*, prevocalic *-iy-* appears before the endings which we find with the consonant stems (§57); cf. the original inflection of the

[12] *-ṇ-* for *-n-* according to §20.

monosyllables in *-ī-* (§51). The following cases of the *vṛkī́*-inflection are foreign to Sanskrit: sing. nom. *vṛk-ī́ḥ* (but cf. *lakṣmīḥ*, etc.); acc. *-yàm* (i.e. *-íy-am*); dat. *-yè*; abl.-gen. *-yàḥ*; loc. *-ī́*. The nom.-acc. dual *-yàu* (also *-yā̀*; see §39) and the nom. plur. *-yàḥ*, on the other hand, agree with *devyau*, *devyaḥ*; these cases of classical Sanskrit are thus taken from the *vṛkī́*-inflection.

The *-ū*-stems are—except for the nom. sing. *-ūḥ*, which agrees not with *dev-ī* but only with *lakṣmīḥ*, Ved. *vṛkī́ḥ*—completely analogous to the *-ī*-stems (cf. §48); we have only to substitute *-u-* for *-i-*, *-ū-* for *-ī-*, *-v-* for *-y-* to transpose these stems from one declension to the other. Historically, as the Ved. language shows, old *-ū-*/*-uv*-stems lie at the basis of these stems (Ved. *tanū́ḥ*, gen. *tanvàḥ* "body, self"), which are of IE origin (cf. Gr. ἰσχῦς, gen. -ύος "strength"); only in the course of the development of the Old Ind. language were they transformed according to the model of the *devī́*-inflection.

(*b*) Monosyllabic

§51. Paradigms *dhī-* f. "understanding," *bhū-* f. "earth."

	Singular	
Nom. Voc.	dhīḥ	bhūḥ
Acc.	dhiyam	bhuvam
Instr.	dhiyā	bhuvā
Dat.	dhiye, dhiyai	bhuve, bhuvai
Abl.	dhiyaḥ, dhiyāḥ	bhuvaḥ, bhuvāḥ
Gen.	dhiyaḥ, dhiyāḥ	bhuvaḥ, bhuvāḥ
Loc.	dhiyi, dhiyām	bhuvi, bhuvām
	Plural	
Nom. Voc.	dhiyaḥ	bhuvaḥ
Acc.	dhiyaḥ	bhuvaḥ
Instr.	dhībhiḥ	bhūbhiḥ
Dat.	dhībhyaḥ	bhūbhyaḥ
Abl.	dhībhyaḥ	bhūbhyaḥ
Gen.	dhiyām, dhīnām	bhuvām, bhūnām
Loc.	dhīṣu	bhūṣu

Dual

Nom. Voc. Acc.	dhiyau	bhuvau
Instr. Dat. Abl.	dhībhyām	bhūbhyām
Gen. Loc.	dhiyoḥ	bhuvoḥ

Exception: *strī-* "woman" forms sing. voc. *stri*, acc. *strīm* beside *striyam*, dat. only *striyai*, abl. gen. only *striyāḥ*, loc. only *striyām*; plur. acc. *strīḥ* beside *striyaḥ*, gen. *strīṇām*. The word thus tends more to the type discussed in §50, in spite of its monosyllabism.

These forms are old monosyllables in *-ī-*, *-ū-*, before vowels *-ii̯-*, *-uu̯-*, with the endings of the type with consonantal stem (§57); cf. Gr. λῖς, nom. plur. λί-ες "lions," ὗς, gen. sing. ὑ-ός "pig," Lat. *sūs*, gen. *su-is* (cf. also the polysyllables in primary *-ī-*, *-ū-* in the Vedic *vṛkī́-* and *tanū́*-type, §50). The double forms (like *dhiy-āḥ* beside *dhiy-aḥ*) are to be ascribed to an influence of the *devī*-inflection (§50).

6. *r*-declension

§52. Paradigm *dātar-* m. n. "giver."

	Singular		Plural	
	m.	n.	m.	n.
Nom.	dātā	dātṛ	dātāraḥ	dātṝṇi[13]
Voc.	dātaḥ	dātṛ, dātaḥ	dātāraḥ	dātṝṇi
Acc.	dātāram	dātṛ	dātṝn	dātṝṇi
Instr.	dātrā	dātṛṇā[13]	dātṛbhiḥ	
Dat.	dātre	dātṛṇe	dātṛbhyaḥ	
Abl.	dātuḥ	dātṛṇaḥ	dātṛbhyaḥ	
Gen.	dātuḥ	dātṛṇaḥ	dātṝṇām	
Loc.	dātari	dātṛṇi	dātṛṣu	

[13] Concerning the *-ṇ-* cf. §20.

	Dual	
	m.	n.
Nom. Voc. Acc.	dātārau	dātṛṇī[13]
Instr. Dat. Abl.	dātṛbhyām	dātṛbhyām
Gen. Loc.	dātroḥ	dātṛṇoḥ

The feminines add -ī- to the weak stem, as in *dātr-ī-* f. "giver, donor"; they are inflected according to the type discussed in § 50.

§ 53. A number of *-r*-stems, above all the kinship names *pitar-* m. "father," *mātar-* f. "mother," *bhrātar-* m. "brother," *duhitar-* f. "daughter" (but not *svasar-* f. "sister," *naptar-* m. "grandson"), as well as *nar-* m. "man," deviate from § 52 in the following cases:

	Singular	Dual	Plural
Nom. Voc.		pitarau	pitaraḥ
Acc.	pitaram	pitarau	

The feminine kinship words in *-r-* have, moreover, the ending *-ṝḥ* (*-s*) in the acc. plur.: *mātṝḥ*, *duhitṝḥ*, *svasṝḥ*.

The gen. plur. of *nar-* "man" also has the form *nṛṇām* beside *nṝṇām*.

Furthermore, in this word from the beginning, cases whose form would have been too short were avoided, like sing. dat. **nr-e*, gen. **nuḥ*. We find instead in Ved. forms in the full grade, sing. dat. *náre*, gen. *nárah*, plur. gen. *narā́m*; later forms of the *-a*-stem *nara-* "man" step into the foreground. The nom.-acc.-voc. dual in (*-ā̆r*)*-au* has the additional form *-ā* in Vedic.

These stems are still rightly treated among the vocalic classes, for they have taken over many characteristics from them: plur. acc. *pitṝn*, f. *mātṝḥ*, gen. *pitṝṇām* conform to *devān* (§ 39), *agnīn* (§ 43), or *senāḥ* (§ 40), *matīḥ* (§ 45) and to *devānām*, *agnīnām*, etc.; they are not cases with consonantal stems like Gr. πατέρ-ας, πατρ-ῶν. But historically the *-r*-stems of the type Lat. *dator*, *datōr-is*, *pater*, *patr-is*

[13] Concerning the *-ṇ-* cf. § 20.

naturally lie at the basis of these forms; the deviation in the stem form noted in §53, e.g. plur. nom. *pitar-aḥ* "fathers," *nar-aḥ* "men," as opposed to *dātār-aḥ* "givers" and *svasār-aḥ* "sisters," is explained as a reflection of the difference in the original vocalic quality, which Gr. πατέρ-ες, ἀνέρ-ες (epic) as opposed to δώτορ-ες, ἔορ-ες (Hesych.) still reveal: cf. §9.

The neuters show, in the same way as the neuter *i*- and *u*-stems (§§46, 48), extension by *-n-* before endings beginning with vowels: like *dātṛ-ṇ-ā*, *vāri-ṇ-ā*, *madhu-n-ā*, etc.

7. Diphthongal Stems

§54. Paradigms *go-* m. f. "cow," *nau-* f. "ship."

	Singular	
N. V.	gauḥ	nauḥ
A.	gām	nāvam
I.	gavā	nāvā
D.	gave	nāve
Ab.	goḥ	nāvaḥ
G.	goḥ	nāvaḥ
L.	gavi	nāvi
	Dual	
N. V. A.	gāvau	nāvau
I. D. Ab.	gobhyām	naubhyām
G. L.	gavoḥ	nāvoḥ
	Plural	
N. V.	gāvaḥ	nāvaḥ
A.	gāḥ	nāvaḥ
I.	gobhiḥ	naubhiḥ
D.	gobhyaḥ	naubhyaḥ
Ab.	gobhyaḥ	naubhyaḥ
G.	gavām	nāvām
L.	goṣu	nauṣu

Cf. sing. *gauḥ*, *gām*, *gavi*, plur. gen. *gav-ām* with Gr. βοῦς, βῶν (Homer., Dor.; cf. §15), βοΐ, βοῶν; sing. *nauḥ*, *nāvam*, *nāvaḥ*, *nāvi*, plur. *nāvaḥ* (nom. and acc.), *nāvām* with Gr. ναῦς/νηῦς, νῆα (Lat. *nāvem*), νηός (Lat. *nāv-is*), νηΐ, νῆες, νῆας, νηῶν.

§55. A diphthongal stem is also shown in the nom.-voc. sing. *dyauḥ* f. "day, sky"; in the remaining cases this word has the stem form *div-* before endings beginning with vowels, *dyu-* before endings beginning with consonants: sing. gen. *div-aḥ*; instr. plur. *dyu-bhiḥ*.

The Vedic language exhibits the inherited, ancient paradigm more clearly: to the sing. nom. *dyáuḥ* (= Gr. Ζεύς) belongs the acc. *dyā́m* (= Gr. Ζῆν, Lat. *diem*; §15), abl.-gen. *dyóḥ* beside *diváḥ* (= Gr. Διός), loc. *dyávi* (= Lat. *Iove*), dual nom.-acc.-voc. *dyā́vā*, plur. nom. *dyā́vaḥ*, acc. *dyū́n*.

§56. A further diphthongal stem, *rai-* m. f. "possession, wealth," is given in the Sanskrit handbooks. But this word does not occur in classical Sanskrit literature; the cited inflection (sing. nom. *rāḥ*, acc. *rāyam*, etc.) appears only in the works of grammarians; Vedic, on the other hand, has preconsonantal *rayí-*, prevocalic *rāy-* (sing. nom. *rayí-ḥ*, acc. *rayí-m*, dat. *rāy-é*, gen. *rāy-áḥ*, etc.), which are clearly from **rə̯-i-*, **reə-i̯-* (**reə-* = root **rē-*, cf. Lat. *rēs*) (§11, 1). Cf. O. Szemerényi, *Zeitschr. f. vergleichende Sprachforschung*, Vol. 73 (1956), pp. 167 ff., with lit.

8. Stems Ending in a Consonant

§57. The declensions of this class, showing every variety of consonantal stem endings, are distinguished by a common system of endings. The case endings for the masculines and feminines are:

	Singular	Dual	Plural
Nom.	—	*-au*	*-aḥ*
Voc.	—		
Acc.	*-am*		

	Singular	Dual	Plural
Instr.	*-ā*	*-bhyām*	*-bhiḥ*
Dat.	*-e*	*-bhyām*	*-bhyaḥ*
Abl.	*-aḥ*	*-bhyām*	*-bhyaḥ*
Gen.	*-aḥ*	*-oḥ*	*-ām*
Loc.	*-i*	*-oḥ*	*-su*

The neuters show no ending in the nom.-voc.-acc. of the sing., *-ī* in the dual, *-i* in the plural (in addition, they usually have nasal or anusvāra before the stem-final consonant; cf. further §60).

These stems remind us of the consonantal stems of the classical languages, which exhibit the same endings after the various stem forms: cf. Lat. *pēs*, *ped-is*; *consul*, *consul-is*; *nōmen*, *nōmin-is*; Gr. φύλαξ, φύλακ-ος; ποιμήν, ποιμέν-ος; νύξ, νυκτ-ός, etc.

The origin of the endings of the consonantal stems: the nom. sing. originally had **-s*, which had to disappear after consonants according to §33, 7; cf. Lat. *pēs* < **pēd+s*. Acc. *-am* < **-m̥*, = Gr. -α (πόδ-α), Lat. *-em* (*ped-em*); dat. *-e* = Lat. *-ī*; abl. gen. *-aḥ* = Gr. -ος or Lat. *-is*; loc. *-i* = Gr. -ι (dat.), Lat. *-e* (abl.).—Plur. nom. *-aḥ* = Gr. -ες; acc. *-aḥ* < **-n̥s* = Gr. -ας, Lat. *-ēs*; gen. *-ām* = Gr. -ων, Lat. *-um*.

§58. With several stems we find the principle of stem gradation. According to it, we must distinguish between strong cases (= nom. voc. acc. singular, nom. voc. acc. dual, nom. voc. plural), middle (= instr. dat. abl. dual, instr. dat. abl. loc. plural), and weakest cases (the rest). Many stems distinguish only between strong and weak cases; to be included among the latter are the "middle" and "weakest" cases of the threefold gradation.

The principle of stem gradation, of ablaut (§36) within a paradigm, is an Indo-European inheritance: cf. Gr. κύ-ων sing. nom., κύ-ον voc., κυ-ν-ός gen. "dog," Goth. *nam-ō* sing. nom., *nam-in* dat., *nam-n-ē* plur. gen. "name," etc.

§59. Stems without Gradation

Paradigms *marut-* m. "wind," *vāc-* f. "word, voice," *jagat-* n. "world."

	Singular		
Nom.-Voc.	marut	vāk	jagat
Acc.	marutam	vācam	jagat
Instr.	marutā	vācā	jagatā
Dat.	marute	vāce	jagate
Abl.-Gen.	marutaḥ	vācaḥ	jagataḥ
Loc.	maruti	vāci	jagati
	Dual		
N. V. A.	marutau	vācau	jagatī
I. D. Ab.	marudbhyām	vāgbhyām	jagadbhyām
G. L.	marutoḥ	vācoḥ	jagatoḥ
	Plural		
N. V. A.	marutaḥ	vācaḥ	jaganti
Instr.	marudbhiḥ	vāgbhiḥ	jagadbhiḥ
Dat. Abl.	marudbhyaḥ	vāgbhyaḥ	jagadbhyaḥ
Gen.	marutām	vācām	jagatām
Loc.	marutsu	vākṣu	jagatsu

Thus the system of endings of §57 is to be used. Some sound-laws are to be noted: assimilation of *-t* to an ending beginning with a voiced sound: *marud-bh°*, *jagad-bh°*, §33 end; *-k* for *-c-* in absolute word-final position (§33, 7) and before *-su*, which becomes *-ṣu* according to §25, or its assimilation to *vāg-bh°*.—The following are inflected similarly: *upaniṣad-* f. "Upanishad," sing. n. *upaniṣat* (§33, 7), a. *upaniṣad-am*, plur. i. *upaniṣad-bhiḥ*, l. *upaniṣat-su*; *sraj-* f. "garland," sing. n. *srak* (§33, 7), a. *sraj-am*, plur. i. *srag-bhiḥ*, l. *srak-ṣu*; *diś-* f. "quarter, region, point of the compass," sing. n. *dik* (§33, 7), a. *diś-am*, plur. i. *dig-bhiḥ*, l. *dik-ṣu*; *dviṣ-* m. "enemy": *dviṭ*, *dviṣam*, *dviḍbhiḥ*, *dviṭsu*; etc.

For *(kāma-)duh-* "milking (wishes)," sing. n. *°dhuk*, a. *°duh-am*, cf. §30, 2 and 33, 7.

Monosyllables in °*r*-, like *gir*- f. "speech," *pur*- f. "city," show a long vowel in the nom. sing. and in the cases whose endings begin with a consonant: sing. n. *gīḥ* (-*r*), a. *gir-am*, plur. i. *gīr-bhiḥ*, g. *gir-ām*, l. *gīr-ṣu*; *pūḥ*, *pur-am*, *pūr-bhiḥ*, *pur-ām*, *pūr-ṣu*.

Historical explanation of this phenomenon, according to §13: *g^{u}*r̥ə̭-s* "song" (from *g^{u}*erə*- "sing" > Ved. *jari-tár*- m. "singer"), *g^{u}*r̥ə̭-bh*° resulted in *gīḥ*, *gīr-bh*°, but *g^{u}*r̥-ə̭-es*, *gir-aḥ* by phonetic laws; the same holds for **pl̥ə̭*- > *pur*- "castle, city."

§60. The neuters in -*as*- also have only one stem. Paradigm *manas*- n. "spirit, mind."

	Singular	Dual	Plural
N. V. A.	manaḥ	manasī	manāṁsi
Instr.	manasā	manobhyām	manobhiḥ
Dat.	manase	manobhyām	manobhyaḥ
Abl.	manasaḥ	manobhyām	manobhyaḥ
Gen.	manasaḥ	manasoḥ	manasām
Loc.	manasi	manasoḥ	manaḥsu

To be noted are: -*o*- for -*as*- (through a stage of *-*az*-) before -*bh*°, cf. §§14 and 33 end; the vowel length in the n. v. a. plur. *man-ā-ṁ-s-i*.

Cf. *manaḥ*, *manas-aḥ*, *manas-i* with Gr. μένος, μένε-ος (μένους), μένε-ϊ, or Lat. *genus* n. "race," *gener-is*, *gener-e* (Old Ind. -*s*- = Gr. -, Lat. -*r*-, §26).

Masculines and feminines in -*as*- form the nom. sing. in -*āḥ*; thus cf. from *su-manas*- adj. "well-disposed":

	Singular	Dual	Plural
Nom.	sumanāḥ	sumanasau	sumanasaḥ
Voc.	sumanaḥ	sumanasau	sumanasaḥ
Acc.	sumanasam	sumanasau	sumanasaḥ
Instr.	sumanasā		

(etc., like *manas*-).

Agreement with Greek also prevails here: cf. °*manāḥ*, *-aḥ*, *-asam*, *-asaḥ* with Gr. εὐ-μενής, -ες, -έα, -έες, -έας.

§61. The neuters in *-iṣ-* and *-uṣ-*, like *jyotiṣ-* "light," *cakṣuṣ-* "eye," are inflected similarly to *manas-*: sing. n. v. a. *jyotiḥ*, *cakṣuḥ*, instr. *jyotiṣ-ā*, *cakṣuṣā*, dual nom. v. a. *jyotiṣī*, plur. n. v. a. *jyotīṁṣi*, etc. Masculines and feminines in *-iṣ-*, *-uṣ-* deviate from the neuters only with respect to the system of endings (§57): cf. *a-cakṣuṣ-* adj. "without sight, blind," sing. nom.-voc. *acakṣuḥ*, acc. *acakṣuṣam*, dual n. v. a. *acakṣuṣau*, plur. n. v. a. *acakṣuṣaḥ*.

§62. Stems with Gradation. The present participles have two stems, a strong stem (§58) in *-ant-*, a weak stem in *-at-*. Thus *bharant-* "bearing":

	Singular	Dual	Plural
N. V.	bharan	bharantau	bharantaḥ
Acc.	bharantam	bharantau	bharataḥ
Instr.	bharatā	bharadbhyām	bharadbhiḥ
etc.			
Neutr. N. V. A.	bharat	bhara(n)tī	bharanti

Cf. the *nt*-participles of the related languages; thus Old Ind. *bharantam*, *-antaḥ* = Gr. φέροντα, -οντες; cf. Lat. *ferens*, Goth. *baírands*, etc.

Reduplicated participles (like *dadat-* "giving") form all cases from the *weak* stem. Nom. v. a. plur. neuter: *dadati* and *dadanti*.

The feminine of the present participles ends in *-ī*, which as a rule is added to the strong stem of thematic verbs (§83), to the weak stem of athematic verbs (§86); declension according to §50.

Further *nt*-formations:

mahānt- "great": strong stem *mahānt-*, weak stem *mahat-*; voc. sing. *mahan*.

Words in *-mant-* and *-vant-* (*mūrtimant-* "having form," *bhagavant-* "exalted") are inflected like *bharant-* but form the nom. sing. in *-mān*, *-vān*; likewise *bhavant-* "your honor, your grace, you," a form of address construed with the 3rd person of the verb.

This form of address probably arose by internal shortening (perhaps like Eng. *miss* < *mistress*, French *sire* < *senior*) from *bhagavant-* "exalted": hence the identity of inflection with the adjectives in *-vant-*, *-mant-*.

Additional Vedic forms with *nt*-formations: n. v. a. dual *-ant-ā* beside *-ant-au*; plur. n. v. a. neutr. *sánti* "being," *paśumánti* (: *paśumánt-* "having cattle"); sing. voc. m. of the words in *-mant-*, *-vant-*: *-maḥ*, *-vaḥ*.

§63. The comparatives in *-īyāṁs-* (§72) are likewise of two stems and have as their weak stem *-īyas-*: sing. nom. *garīyān* "heavier," acc. *garīyāṁs-am*, instr. *garīyas-ā*, plur. instr. *garīyo-bhiḥ*,[14] etc.

§64. The adjectives in *-añc-* are partly of two stems, like *prāñc-* "eastern," weak stem *prāc-*; *avāñc-* "downward," weak stem *avāc-*; partly of three stems, cf. *udañc-* "northern," middle stem *udac-*, weakest stem *udīc-*; *pratyañc-* "western," middle stem *pratyac-*, weakest stem *pratīc-*; *nyañc-* "low," middle stem *nyac-*, weakest stem *nīc-*; *anvañc-* "following," middle stem *anvac-*, weakest stem *anūc-*; *tiryañc-* "going aside," middle stem *tiryac-*, weakest stem *tiraśc-*: sing. nom. *prāṅ*, *pratyaṅ*, instr. *prācā*, *pratīcā*, plur. instr. *prāgbhiḥ*, *pratyagbhiḥ*, etc.

For the historical explanation see Wackernagel–Debrunner, *Altind. Grammatik*, Vol. III (1930), pp. 229 ff.; W. Morgenroth, *Archiv Orientální*, Vol. 29 (1961), pp. 575 ff., with lit.

[14] *-o-* from *-az-* according to §§14, 33 (end).

n-stems

§65. Paradigms *rājan-* m. "king," *nāman-* n. "name."

	Singular	
Nom.	rājā	nāma
Voc.	rājan	nāma
Acc.	rājānam	nāma
Instr.	rājñā[15]	nāmnā
Dat.	rājñe	nāmne
Abl.	rājñaḥ	nāmnaḥ
Gen.	rājñaḥ	nāmnaḥ
Loc.	rājñi, rājani	nāmni, nāmani
	Dual	
N. V. A.	rājānau	nāmnī, nāmanī
I. D. Ab.	rājabhyām	nāmabhyām
G. L.	rājñoḥ	nāmnoḥ
	Plural	
Nom.	rājānaḥ	nāmāni
Voc.	rājānaḥ	nāmāni
Acc.	rājñaḥ	nāmāni
Instr.	rājabhiḥ	nāmabhiḥ
Dat.	rājabhyaḥ	nāmabhyaḥ
Abl.	rājabhyaḥ	nāmabhyaḥ
Gen.	rājñām	nāmnām
Loc.	rājasu	nāmasu

Thus the strong stem ends in *-ān-*, the middle stem in *-a-*, the weakest stem in *-n-*.

Historically the *-a-* of the middle stem (*rāj-a-bhiḥ*) is naturally to be derived from *-*n̥*- (§8); *rāj-a-* and *rāj-ñ-* are thus the same in origin.

[15] *-n-* immediately after *-j-* becomes *-ñ-* by phonetic law.

Words in which more than one consonant precedes the *-an-*, e.g. *ātman-* m. "soul," *brahman-* n. "Brahman," show the stem form *-an-* instead of *-n-* in the weakest cases: sing. instr. *ātmanā*, *brahmaṇā* (§20), etc.

Thus forms like **ātmnā* which are contrary to structure have been avoided.

The names of gods *Pūṣan-* m. and *Aryaman-* m., as well as compounds in *-han-* "killing" (like *vṛtra-han-* "slayer of Vṛtra"), show *-an-* with a short vowel in stem-final position in the sing. acc., dual nom.-voc.-acc., and plur. nom.: *Pūṣaṇam*, *vṛtrahaṇam*. The formations in *-han-* occur in the classical language mostly in the nom. sing.; sporadic examples of the "weakest" cases show the full grade carried through: sing. instr. *vṛtra-haṇā*, gen. *brahma-haṇaḥ* "of the slayer of Brahmans."

In Vedic an ablauting paradigm preceded this, e.g. sing. nom. *vṛtra-hā́*, acc. *-háṇam*, dat. *-ghné*, gen. *-ghnáḥ*, etc. (*-gh-*: §27). But this is—except for the singular *-ghnaḥ* in Manu—no longer Sanskrit usage.

The words *śvan-* m. "dog," *maghavan-* m. "Indra," *yuvan-* "young, youth" are inflected like *rājan-*; their weakest cases have the stem forms *śun-*, *maghon-*, *yūn-*: sing. nom. *śvā*, *maghavā*, *yuvā*, voc. *śvan*, *maghavan*, *yuvan*, acc. *śvānam*, *maghavānam*, *yuvānam*, instr. *śunā*, *maghonā*, *yūnā*, etc.

Additional forms of the *-an*-stems from Vedic are worthy of mention: 1. the occurrence of "endingless" locatives (without *-i*), e.g. *mūrdhán* "on the head" beside *mūrdháni*; 2. neuter nom.-voc.-acc. plur. in *-ā*, *-a*: *nā́mā*, *nā́ma* beside *nā́māni*; 3. dual nom.-voc.-acc. (*-ān*)*-ā* beside *-au*; cf. especially *yū́nā* beside *yúvānā*.

For comparison the *n*-stems of the related languages, such as Lat. *homo*, *homin-is*, Goth. *guma*, *gumin-s*, should be cited. The threefold stem gradation of Old Ind. is an IE inheritance: cf. Old Ind. *-ān-*, *-an-*, and *-n-/-a-* (< **-n̥-*) with Gr. ποι-μήν, ποι-μέν-ος, ποί-μν-η and ποιμαίνω < *ποι-μn̥-i̯ω. Old Ind. *-ān-* in *rāj-ān-am*, *-ān-au*, *-ān-aḥ*, of course, must not have been the IE length, but *-ŏ- according to §9; the endings thus would correspond to Gr. (τέκτ)ονα, -ονες and stand opposed to *-han-am*, *-han-aḥ*, which, on account of *h*, are explainable only from **gᵘhen-m̥*, *-es* (§27). For something similar see §53.

The same ablaut forms after *-v-*, Old Ind. *-vān-*, *-van-*, *-un-*, *-va-*, IE *-u̯ōn-*, *-u̯on-*, *-un-*, *-u̯n̥-*, explain Old Ind. *śvān-*, *śvan*, *śun-*, *śva-*, Gr. κύων, κύον, κυν-, but also *magha-van-*: **magha-un-* (> *maghon-* §14), *yuvan-*: *yūn-* (**yu-un-*).

§66. The word for "way, path" shows partial inflection according to the *-n*-stems: sing. acc. *panthānam*, plur. nom.-voc. *panthānaḥ*; the nom. sing. is *panthāḥ*; the middle cases are formed from *pathi-* (e.g. plur. instr. *pathibhiḥ*), the weakest cases from *path-* (sing. gen. *pathaḥ*).

ahan- n. "day" forms the nom.-voc.-acc. sing. from a stem *ahar-*, the middle cases from *ahas-*: sing. nom. *ahaḥ* (*-r*), instr. *ahnā*, plur. instr. *aho-bhiḥ* (< **ahaz-bh°*, §14), loc. *ahaḥ-su*.

Also to be mentioned are the nouns with a mixed inflection of *-i-* and *-n*-stems; see §47.

The *-n*-form *panthān-* (certainly already old) arose under the influence of the synonym *adhvan-* "way"; the oldest Ved. inflection is sing. n. *pánthāḥ*, acc. *pánthām*, gen. *patháḥ*, plur. i. *pathíbhiḥ*; this continues an archaic paradigm **pónt-ēs*, **pónt-ē-m*, **pn̥t-ə̯-és*, **pn̥t-ə-bhis*, cf. §11, 2. The grammarians, but not the literary texts, still know similarly inflected *manthān-* "whisk" and *r̥bhukṣān-* "a divine being." *ahan-/ahar-/ahas-* is also an archaism, a "heteroclite," of somewhat the same type as Lat. *femur*, *femin-is*, etc.

§67. Stems in *-in-*: Paradigm *hastin-* m. "elephant."

	Singular	Dual	Plural
Nom.	hastī	hastinau	hastinaḥ
Voc.	hastin	hastinau	hastinaḥ
Acc.	hastinam	hastinau	hastinaḥ

	Singular	Dual	Plural
Instr.	hastinā	hastibhyām	hastibhiḥ
Dat.	hastine	hastibhyām	hastibhyaḥ
Abl.	hastinaḥ	hastibhyām	hastibhyaḥ
Gen.	hastinaḥ	hastinoḥ	hastinām
Loc.	hastini	hastinoḥ	hastiṣu

The neuters of adjectives in *-in-* (*balin-* "mighty") deviate from the masc. in the following cases: sing. n. a. *bali*, v. *bali*, *balin*; dual n. v. a. *balinī*; plur. n. v. a. *balīni*.

The feminine of such adjectives ends in *-ī*: *balin-ī*; inflection according to §50.

-in- is really the zero grade of a stem-formation suffix, Old Ind. *-yan-* (: Lat. *leg-iōn-*), probably still preserved in Ved. *kan-yán-ām* "a virgin," but the old ablaut has completely disappeared, and *-ī*, *-i-bhiḥ*, *-īni*, etc. have been created according to the genuinely ablauting model of *-ā*, *-a-bhiḥ* (< *-n̥-), *-āni* (§65).

Ved.: Nom.-voc.-acc. dual *-in-ā* beside *-in-au*.

§68. The perfect active participles in *-vas-* (*vidvas-* "knowing") show as their strong stem *vidvāṁs-* (sing. nom. *vidvān*, voc. *vidvan*, acc. *vidvāṁs-am*), as their middle stem *vidvat-* (plur. instr. *vidvadbhiḥ*, loc. *vidvatsu*), as their weakest stem *viduṣ-* (sing. instr. *viduṣā*). Neuter nom. sing. *vidvat*, dual *viduṣī*, plur. *vidvāṁsi*. Fem. *viduṣī-* (declined according to §50).

In Vedic the voc. sing. m. has the ending *-vaḥ* beside *-van*.

Cf. Gr. εἰδώς, εἰδότ-ος (ϝειδ-ϝότ-) "knowing," Goth. *weit-wōd-* m. "witness" (: Old Ind. *vid-vat-*, *vid-vā[ṁ]s-*), f. Homer. ἰδυῖα < *ϝιδυσ-ια (= *viduṣ-ī*).

§69. *ap-* f. "water" is used only in the plural in Sanskrit: nom. *āp-aḥ*, acc. *ap-aḥ*, instr. *ad-bhiḥ*, dat.-abl. *ad-bhyaḥ*, gen. *ap-ām*, loc. *ap-su*.

Singular forms also occur sporadically in Vedic (instr. *ap-ā́*, gen. *ap-áḥ*).—*ad-bh°* is dissimilated for **ab-bh°*, **ap-bh°*.

§70. *puṁs-* m. "man" has as its strong stem *pumāṁs-*, as its middle stem *pum-*, as its weak stem *puṁs-*: sg. nom. *pumān*, voc. *puman*, acc. *pumāṁs-am*, instr. *puṁs-ā*, plur. instr. *pum-bhiḥ*.

anaḍ-vah- m. "ox" has the strong stem *anaḍvah-*, but sing. nom. *anaḍvān*, voc. *anaḍvan*; middle stem *anaḍut-*; weakest stem *anaḍuh-*.

Comparison of Adjectives

§71. The usual suffix for the comparative is *-tara-* (f. *-tarā-*), for the superlative *-tama-* (f. *-tamā-*); these suffixes are added to the pure stem of the adjective, with twofold stem gradation to the weak stem, with threefold stem gradation to the middle stem (§58). Examples: *priya-* "dear" (§41): comp. *priya-tara-*, sup. *priya-tama-*; *mahānt-* "great" (§62): comp. *mahat-tara-*, sup. *mahat-tama-*; *vidvas-* "knowing" (§68): comp. *vidvat-tara-*, sup. *vidvat-tama-*.

The forms of comparison are inflected according to §41.

In Vedic the use of the weakest stem form also occurs: *vidúṣ-ṭara-* comp.

Cf. with *-tara-* Gr. πιστό-τερο-ς, with *-tama-* especially Lat. *in-timus*, *ul-timus*.

§72. A less common means of comparison adds the suffixes *-īyāṁs-* for the comparative, *-iṣṭha-* (f. *-iṣṭhā-*) for the superlative, directly to the root of the adjective, usually in its guṇa-grade form. Cf.:

alpa- "little, small": comp. *alp-īyāṁs-*, sup. *alp-iṣṭha-*;
mṛdu- "soft": comp. *mrad-īyāṁs-*, *mrad-iṣṭha-*;
yuvan- "young": comp. *yav-īyāṁs-*, *yav-iṣṭha-*;
kṣipra- "quick": comp. *kṣep-īyāṁs-*, *kṣep-iṣṭha-*; etc.

Inflection of the comparatives according to §63, of the superlatives according to §41.

Beside *-īyāṁs-*, *-īyas-*, *-yas-* (Ved. *náv-yas-* "newer") is also found in the older language; it is the continuation of a richly ablauting IE **-i̯es-*, **-i̯os-*, lengthened grade **-i̯ōs-*, zero grade **-is-* (§36); cf. Lat.

ma-ies-tas, *ma-ius*, *ma-iōr-em*, *mag-is*; *-ī-yas-* is specifically to be compared with Gr. ἡδ-ίω, ἡδ-ίους. Sup. *-iṣṭha-* = Gr. ἥδ-ιστο-ς, Goth. *reik-ist-s* "mightiest," Eng. *-est* in *rich-est*.

2. The Pronoun

§73. Personal pronouns

	1st person	2nd person
	Singular	
	"I"	"you"
Nom. V.	aham	tvam
Acc.	mām, mā[16]	tvām, tvā
Instr.	mayā	tvayā
Dat.	mahyam, me	tubhyam, te
Abl.	mat	tvat
Gen.	mama, me	tava, te
Loc.	mayi	tvayi
	Dual	
	"we two"	"you two"
N. V. A.	āvām	yuvām
I. D. Ab.	āvābhyām	yuvābhyām
G. L.	āvayoḥ	yuvayoḥ
	Plural	
	"we"	"you"
Nom. V.	vayam	yūyam
Acc.	asmān, naḥ	yuṣmān, vaḥ
Instr.	asmābhiḥ	yuṣmābhiḥ
Dat.	asmabhyam, naḥ	yuṣmabhyam, vaḥ
Abl.	asmat	yuṣmat
Gen.	asmākam, naḥ	yuṣmākam, vaḥ
Loc.	asmāsu	yuṣmāsu

[16] The forms written second (*mā*, *tvā*, *naḥ*, etc.) are enclitics.

Enclitic for the acc. dat. gen. dual of the 1st person: *nau*, 2nd person: *vām*.

The following forms are used as stems, since they are the forms found in compounds involving these words (§ 141): *mad-* for "I," *asmad-* for "we," *tvad-* for "you (sg.)," *yuṣmad-* for "you (pl.)."

Instead of the 2nd person of the personal pronoun *bhavant-* is used in polite address; see § 62, p. 55.

Special forms of the older language: 2nd pers. sing. instr. *tvā́*, loc. *tvé*; plur. dat.-gen.-loc. 1st per. *asmé*, 2nd pers. *yuṣmé*; dual nom. 1st p. *āvám*, 2nd p. *yuvám*; instr. 2nd p. *yuvā́bhyām*; abl. 1st p. *āvát*, 2nd p. *yuvát*; gen.-loc. 2nd p. *yuvóḥ*.

Compare *ah-am*, *mām*, *mahy-am* with Lat. *ego*, *me*, *mihi*; encl. *me* = Gr. μοι; *tv-am*, *tubhy-am* ~ Lat. *tu*, *tibi*; encl. *te* = Gr. τοι; *vay-am* ~ Goth. *wei-s*, Ger. *wir*; *asma°* = proto-Greek *ἀσμέ > Aeol.-Homer. ἄμμε, Ion.-Att. ἡμέας; encl. *naḥ* ~ Lat. *nōs*, Goth. Ger. *uns* (**n̥s*); *yū-yam* ~ Goth. *jus*; *y-uṣma°* = proto-Greek *ὐσμέ- > Aeol.-Homer. ὔμμε, Ion.-Att. ῡ̔μέας; encl. *vaḥ* ~ Lat. *vōs*.

Demonstratives

§ 74. Stem *tad-* "this, he."

	Singular		Dual	
	m.	f.	m.	f.
Nom.	saḥ	sā	tau	te
Acc.	tam	tām	tau	te
Instr.	tena	tayā	tābhyām	
Dat.	tasmai	tasyai	tābhyām	
Abl.	tasmāt	tasyāḥ	tābhyām	
Gen.	tasya	tasyāḥ	tayoḥ	
Loc.	tasmin	tasyām	tayoḥ	

	Plural	
	m.	f.
Nom.	te	tāḥ
Acc.	tān	tāḥ
Instr.	taiḥ	tābhiḥ
Dat.	tebhyaḥ	tābhyaḥ
Abl.	tebhyaḥ	tābhyaḥ
Gen.	teṣām	tāsām
Loc.	teṣu	tāsu

Neuter n. a. sing. *tat*, dual *te*, plural *tāni*, otherwise as in the masc.

etad- "this" is declined likewise: *eṣaḥ*,[17] *eṣā*, *etat*, acc. *etam*, *etām*, *etat*, etc.

The nom. sing. m. *saḥ* (*eṣaḥ*) appears in this form only in absolute word-final position; in sandhi before *a-*, *so*, *eṣo* appears, and *a-* is elided (§33, 12*c*). Before all remaining initial sounds we have *sa*, *eṣa*; a possible hiatus remains.

Additional forms of the Vedic language: m. sing. instr. *ténā*, loc. *sásmin*, dual nom.-acc. *tā́*, plur. instr. *tébhiḥ*; n. plur. nom.-acc. *tā́*.

Old Ind. *sa* (this form, preferred in sandhi [see above], is more ancient than the form in absolute word-final position, *saḥ*) = Gr. ὁ, Goth. *sa*; acc. *tam* = Gr. τόν, Goth. *þan-a*: the Old Ind. alternation between *sa-* and *ta-*stem in this paradigm is thus an IE inheritance.—Cf. further: Old Ind. *tasm°* ~ Goth. *þamma*; *tasya* = Gr. τοῖο; f. *sā* = Gr. ἡ, Goth. *sō*; acc. *tām* = Gr. τήν, Goth. *þō*; *tasyai*, *tasyāḥ* ~ Goth. *þizai*, *þizōs*; n. *tat* = Gr. τό, Lat. *is-tud*, Goth. *þat-a*. Plur. m. *te* = Dor. Gr. τοί, Goth. *þai*; f. gen. *tāsām* = Lat. *is-tārum*; etc.

§75. A demonstrative stem *ena-* "that, he" appears only in the accusative case of the three numbers (sing. *enam* m., *enām* f., *enat* n.; dual *enau*, *ene*, *ene*; plur. *enān*, *enāḥ*, *enāni*), in the instrumental sing. (*enena*, *enayā*), and in the gen.-loc. dual (*enayoḥ*).

In Ved.: gen.-loc. dual *enoḥ*.

[17] Cf. §25.

§76. Stem *idam-* "this."

	Singular		Dual	
	m.	f.	m.	f.
Nom.	ayam	iyam	imau	ime
Acc.	imam	imām	imau	ime
Instr.	anena	anayā	ābhyām	
Dat.	asmai	asyai	ābhyām	
Abl.	asmāt	asyāḥ	ābhyām	
Gen.	asya	asyāḥ	anayoḥ	
Loc.	asmin	asyām	anayoḥ	

	Plural	
	m.	f.
Nom.	ime	imāḥ
Acc.	imān	imāḥ
Instr.	ebhiḥ	ābhiḥ
Dat.	ebhyaḥ	ābhyaḥ
Abl.	ebhyaḥ	ābhyaḥ
Gen.	eṣām	āsām
Loc.	eṣu	āsu

Neuter n. a. sing. *idam*, dual *ime*, plur. *imāni*, otherwise as in the masc.

Additional forms of Vedic: sing. instr. m. n. *enā́*, f. *ayā́*; gen. m. n. *imásya*; dual m. nom.-acc. *imā́*; gen.-loc. *ayóḥ*; plur. nom.-acc. n. *imā́*.

Old Ind. *ay-am*, *iy-am*, *id-am* belong to the IE pronominal stem of Lat. *i-s*, *i-d* (=Old Ind. *id-am*); in addition, the acc. *im-am*, originally **i-m+-am*, from which a "stem *ima-*" was early abstracted: *imām*, *imau*, *ime*, *imān*, etc.—Other cases are formed from the Old Ind. stems *a-* and *ana-*.

§77. Stem *adas-* "that."

	Singular		Dual
	m.	f.	m. f. n.
Nom.	asau	asau	amū
Acc.	amum	amūm	amū
Instr.	amunā	amuyā	amūbhyām
Dat.	amuṣmai	amuṣyai	amūbhyām
Abl.	amuṣmāt	amuṣyāḥ	amūbhyām
Gen.	amuṣya	amuṣyāḥ	amuyoḥ
Loc.	amuṣmin	amuṣyām	amuyoḥ

	Plural	
	m.	f.
Nom.	amī	amūḥ
Acc.	amūn	amūḥ
Instr.	amībhiḥ	amūbhiḥ
Dat.	amībhyaḥ	amūbhyaḥ
Abl.	amībhyaḥ	amūbhyaḥ
Gen.	amīṣām	amūṣām
Loc.	amīṣu	amūṣu

The neuter differs from the masc. only in the n. a. sing. *adaḥ* and plural *amūni*.

In Vedic the nom.-acc. plur. n. also occurs in the form *amū́*. With *a-sau* cf. Gr. οὗ-τος, αὕ-τη. The historical explanation of the rest is complicated: Cf. Chr. Hauri, *Zeitschr. f. vergleichende Sprachforschung*, Vol. 78 (1963), pp. 115 ff. and the lit. mentioned there.

§78. Most additional pronouns are inflected like *tad-*, §74:

1. The relative *yad-* "which": sing. nom. m. *yaḥ*, f. *yā*, n. *yat*, acc. *yam*, *yām*, *yat*, instr. *yena*, etc.

Identical with Gr. ὅς, ἥ, ὅ.

2. The interrogative *kim-* "which, who?": sing. nom. *kaḥ*, *kā*, *kim* irregular in the neutr.; acc. *kam*, *kām*, *kim*; inst. *kena*, etc.—Indefinites are formed by addition of *cit*, *cana*, or *api* to the forms of the interrogative: sing. nom. m. *kaś-cit*, *kaś-cana*, *ko 'pi* "anyone" (§33, 12*a*, *c*), n. *kiṁ-cit*, *kiṁ-cana*, *kim-api* "anything."

Old Ind. *ka-* = IE *q^uo- in Lat. *quo-d*, Goth. *hvas* "who."

3. The pronominal adjectives *anya-* "other," *itara-* "other." The following pronouns or pronominal adjectives and numerals are declined, in the nom.-acc. sing. n., in *-am*, otherwise according to §74: *eka-* "one" (*ekaḥ*, *ekā*, *ekam*; §79); *ekatara-* "one of two"; *ubhaya-*(f. *-ī-*) "both"; *viśva-* "whole"; *sarva-* "all"; likewise the following, which, however, can also form the abl. loc. sing. m. n. and nom. plur. m. according to the *a*-stems (§39): *adhara-* "lower" (nom. plur. m. *adhare* and *adharāḥ*, etc.), *antara-* "inner," *apara-* "other," *avara-* "posterior, western," *dakṣiṇa-* "on the right," *para-* "later," *pūrva-* "earlier," *sva-* "own, one's own," *uttara-* "upper."

3. The Numeral

§79. Cardinals

1. *eka-* "one" is inflected according to §78, 3.

2. *dvi-* "two": dual inflection, n. v. a. m. *dvau*, f. n. *dve*; i. d. ab. *dvābhyām*, g. l. *dvayoḥ*.

In Vedic beside *d(u)váu* we also find *d(u)vā́*; = Homeric Gr. δύω, Lat. *duo*.

3. *tri-* "three" has the following inflection:

	m.	n.	f.
N. V.	trayaḥ	trīṇi	tisraḥ
Acc.	trīn	trīṇi	tisraḥ
Instr.	tribhiḥ		tisṛbhiḥ

	m. n.	f.
Dat. Abl.	tribhyaḥ	tisṛbhyaḥ
Gen.	trayāṇām	tisṛṇām
Loc.	triṣu	tisṛṣu

Additional forms in Vedic: nom.-acc. n. *trī́*; gen. m. *trīṇā́m*.

Old Ind. *trayaḥ* = Gr. τρεῖς, Lat. *trēs*, Goth. *þreis*; Ved. *trī́* = OCS *tri*; *tribhyaḥ*, *triṣu* ~ Lat. *tribus*, Gr. τρισί. The feminines *tisr*° (for **tri-sr*°) and *catasr*° (see the following) continue archaisms which occur only in the "border languages" of Indo-European, Indo-Iranian and Celtic; cf. Old Irish *teoir* "three (f.)," *cetheoir* "four (f.)."

4. *catur-* "four" is inflected as follows:

	m.	n.	f.
N. V.	catvāraḥ	catvāri	catasraḥ
Acc.	caturaḥ	catvāri	catasraḥ
Instr.	caturbhiḥ		catasṛbhiḥ
Dat. Abl.	caturbhyaḥ		catasṛbhyaḥ
Gen.	caturṇām		catasṛṇām
Loc.	caturṣu		catasṛṣu

This word is cognate with Gr. τέτταρες, τέσσαρες, Lat. *quattuor*, etc.; concerning the special feminine formation see the preceding.

5. *pañca* "five" is declined in the n. v. a. *pañca*, instr. *pañcabhiḥ*, d. ab. *pañcabhyaḥ*, g. *pañcānām*, l. *pañcasu*.

As the lack of an ending in the n. v. a. and the still optional use of the inflected forms in Vedic show, *pañca* (= Gr. πέντε, Lat. *quīnque*) was originally indeclinable; the same holds for the following numerals, 6 and 7 (identical with Lat. *sex*, *septem*), 9 and 10 (= Lat. *novem*, *decem*). Concerning 8 see below.

6. *ṣaṣ* "six" has the inflection n. v. a. *ṣaṭ*, instr. *ṣaḍbhiḥ*, d. ab. *ṣaḍbhyaḥ*, gen. *ṣaṇṇām*, loc. *ṣaṭsu*.

7. *sapta* "seven" is inflected like *pañca* (5).

8. *aṣṭa* "eight" can be inflected like *pañca*, but the following inflection is also possible: n. v. a. *aṣṭau*, instr. *aṣṭābhiḥ*, d. ab. *aṣṭābhyaḥ*, gen. *aṣṭānām*, loc. *aṣṭāsu*.

In Vedic beside *aṣṭáu* (=Goth. *ahtau*) we also find *aṣṭā́* (=Gr. ὀκτώ, Lat. *octō*).

9. *nava* "nine": inflected like *pañca*.
10. *daśa* "ten": inflected like *pañca*.

The remaining cardinal numbers: *ekādaśa* "11," *dvādaśa* "12," *trayodaśa* "13," *caturdaśa* "14," *pañcadaśa* "15," *ṣoḍaśa* "16," *saptadaśa* "17," *aṣṭādaśa* "18," *navadaśa* or *ūnaviṁśatiḥ* "19," *viṁśatiḥ* (fem. *i*-stem) "20," *triṁśat* (f.) "30," *catvāriṁśat* "40," *pañcāśat* "50," *ṣaṣṭiḥ* (f. *i*-stem) "60," *saptatiḥ* "70," *aśītiḥ* "80," *navatiḥ* "90," *śatam* (n. *a*-stem) "100."

dve śate or *dviśatam*, *trīṇi śatāni* or *triśatam* "200, 300"; *sahasram* "1000"; *lakṣam* "100,000."

§80. Ordinals

1. *prathama-* "first";
2. *dvitīya-*;
3. *tṛtīya-*;
4. *caturtha-*, *turīya-*;
5. *pañcama-*;
6. *ṣaṣṭha-*;
7. *saptama-*;
8. *aṣṭama-*;
9. *navama-*;
10. *daśama-*;

11. *ekādaśa-*, 12. *dvādaśa-*, 20. *viṁśa-* or *viṁśatitama-*, 30. *triṁśa-*, *triṁśat-tama-*, etc.; 60. only *ṣaṣṭitama-* (but 61. *ekaṣaṣṭitama-* and *ekaṣaṣṭa-*), 100. *śatatama-*, 1000. *sahasratama-*.

In Vedic *pañcathá-* "fifth," *saptathá-* "seventh" also occur.—Cf. *tṛtīya-* with Lat. *tertius*; *caturtha-* with Gr. τέταρτος; *ṣaṣṭha-* with Lat. *sextus*; *saptama-* and *daśama-* with *septimus*, *decimus*.

§81. Numeral Adverbs

sakṛt "once," *dviḥ* "twice," *triḥ* "three times," *catuḥ* "four times," *pañca-kṛtvaḥ* "five times," *ṣaṭ-kṛtvaḥ* "six times"; etc.

ekadhā "in one way," *dvi-* or *dvedhā* "in two ways," *tri-*, *tredhā* "in three ways," *caturdhā* "in four ways," *bahudhā* "in many ways"; etc.

ekaśaḥ "individually," *dviśáḥ* "in twos," *triśaḥ* "in threes," *śataśaḥ* "in 100s," etc.

sa-kṛt < **sm̥-* (§8), ~ Lat. *sem-el*, Gr. ἅ-παξ < **sm̥-*; *dviḥ* = Gr. δίς, Lat. *bis* (old *duis*); *triḥ* = Gr. τρίς, Lat. *ter*; *catuḥ* ~ Lat. *quater*.—With (*eka*)-*śaḥ* cf. Homeric Gr. ἀνδρα-κάς "man for man."

4. The Verb

§82. Sanskrit distinguishes the following voices: active, middle,[18] and passive (§128). Tenses: present, imperfect, aorist, perfect, future (and conditional). There are three moods: indicative, optative, and imperative.

The forms of the present and imperfect are derived from a special *present stem* built on the *root*, from which, on the other hand, special stems for the remaining tenses are formed. We distinguish two large principal groups, thematic and athematic verbs, according to the formation of the present stems, and within these groups ten classes postulated by the Old Ind. grammarians.

(*a*) Thematic Verbs (Classes 1, 4, 6, 10)

§83. The conjugation of these classes (§84) is completely uniform. The only differences are in the way in which the present stems are formed from the root:

1st class: The root[19] is guṇated (§35) and appears before the "thematic vowel" *-a-* (*-ā-*) and the ending: root *bhṛ-* "bear," *ruh-* "grow," guṇa *bhar-*, *roh-*, 3rd person sing. *bhar-a-ti* "he

[18] The Old Ind. grammarians designate the active as *parasmaipada* ("form for the other"), the middle as *ātmanepada* ("form for oneself").

[19] Sanskrit dictionaries usually do not list verbs under a finite form, but under the root, with citation of the present class: thus not *bharati* "bears," but *bhṛ-* cl. 1, p. (= parasmaipada, active) "bear."

bears," *roh-a-ti* "he grows." Roots in final *-ĭ*, *-ŭ*, like *nī-* "lead," *bhū-* "become," show the guṇa form (*ne-*, *bho-*) decomposed into *-ay-*, *-av-* before the thematic vowel (according to §§5, 14): *nay-a-ti* "he leads," *bhav-a-ti* "he becomes."

IE thematic type with *-e*-grade: Gr. φέρ-ω, λείπ-ω, Lat. *leg-ō*, etc.

Roots with a long closed syllable, like *jīv-* "live," *nind-* "blame," show no guṇation: *jīvati* "he lives," *nindati* "he blames."

The following present formations are also assigned to class I as "exceptions": *gam-* "go," *gacchati*; *yam-* "curb," *yacchati.*—*kram-* "step", *krāmati* (middle *kramate*); *cam-* (with *ā-*) "sip," *cāmati*; *guh-* "hide," *gūhati.*—*daṁś-* "bite," *daśati.*—*ghrā-* "smell," *jighrati*; *pā-* "drink," *pibati*; *sthā-* "stand," *tiṣṭhati*; *sad-* "sit," *sīdati.*

In part these are special IE present classes which have no special place in the 10-class system of the Indians; verbs like *ga-ccha-ti* belong to the *-sk̂-* presents, Gr. -σκω, Lat. *-scō*, §18; *ji-ghra-ti*, *ti-ṣṭha-ti*, etc. are thematized reduplicating presents like Gr. γί-γν-ο-μαι, Lat. *gi-gn-ō*.

4th Class: *-ya-* and the ending are added to the unchanged root. Root *kup-* "be angry," *kup-ya-ti* "he is angry"; *nah-* "bind," *nah-ya-ti* "he binds."

IE *-i̯*-presents, like Lat. *cup-i-ō*.

Peculiarities of class 4: *tam-* "become numb," *bhram-* "wander," *śam-* "become quiet," *śram-* "become tired" form the present stem in °*ām-ya-* (e.g. *tām-ya-ti*); *mad-* "rejoice" forms *mād-ya-ti*. To *jan-* "be born" belongs the deponent *jā-ya-te*. *vyadh-* "bore through": *vidh-ya-ti*; *śā-* "whet," *sā-* "bind, decide": *śyati*, *syati*. To *bhraṁś-* "fall" and *rañj-* "get red" belong the present stems *bhraś-ya-* *raj-ya-*.—*paś-ya-ti* "sees" is supplied as the present of the unrelated root *dṛś-* "see."

°*ām-ya-* is the present stem of roots in °*mə̥-*; *jā-yate* is **ǵn̥ə-i̯-* (concerning the seṭ-root in *jani-tár-*, §§9, 37). In *bhraś-ya-*, as opposed to *bhraṁś-*, *-a-* is old *-n̥- (§8). *paś-ya-* and *dṛś-* are the cognates of Lat. *speciō* and Gr. δέρκομαι.

6th Class: The thematic vowel is added to the root, which is not guṇated; cf. *tud-* "push," *tud-a-ti* "he pushes"; *kṣip-* "throw," *kṣipati* "he throws."

These presents bear the accent on the thematic vowel in Vedic (*tudáti*).

The following are placed here as special formations: *iṣ-* "wish," *praś-* "ask," *ṛ-* "go, move," presents *icchati*, *pṛcchati*, *ṛcchati*; *kṛt-* "cut," *muc-* "release," *lip-* "besmear," *lup-* "plunder," *vid-* "find," *sic-* "sprinkle," presents *kṛntati*, *muñcati*, *limpati*, *lumpati*, *vindati*, *siñcati*.—*kṝ-* "scatter," *kir-a-ti*.

The first are again *-sk̑-* presents (see under 1); *kṛt-* etc. form nasal-infixing thematic presents, like Lat. *sci-n-d-ō*, *rumpō*. *kir-á-* from **kr̥ə-é-*, §13.

10th Class: *-ay-* appears between root and thematic vowel; roots with medial *-i-*, *-u-*, *-ṛ-* before simple consonants are guṇated: cf. *cur-* "steal," guṇa *cor-*, present *cor-ay-a-ti* "he steals."—Sometimes the weak grade of the root also occurs (*pīḍ-* "torture": *pīḍayati*).—In cases where an *-a-* separated from *-aya-* by only one consonant would normally develop in the root by guṇation, as a rule *-ā-* appears here instead, but this is not always true. This can be gathered, above all, from the rather frequent formation of the causatives (§129), whose basic type is identical with that of the 10th class: cf. root *bhū-* "become," guṇa *bho-*, prevocalic *bhav-* (§§5, 14), but causative *bhāv-aya-ti*; *kṛ-* "make," causative *kārayati*; *sad-* "sit," *sādayati*. On the other hand we have *jan-* "beget": *janayati*, *dam-* "tame": *damayati*, etc.

The IE basic type had *-o*-grade of the root and *-ei̯-* before the thematic vowel: cf. Gr. ποτ-έ-ομαι, Lat. *mon-e-ō*, Goth. caus. *satja* "cause to sit, set" (**sod-ei̯-ō*). The frequent Old Ind. type with *-ā-* in an open root syllable (*kārayati*) is partly explained by lengthened grade already existing in IE (: Gr. πωτάομαι), but partly also by the law given in §9, which also explains the preserved normal grade in *janayati*, etc. (: seṭ-root *jan^{i}-*). The created models have naturally been generalized over the phonetic laws.

Conjugation

§84. Paradigm *bhṛ-* I (= 1st class) "bear."

Present Active Indicative

	Singular	Dual	Plural
1st	bharāmi	bharāvaḥ	bharāmaḥ
2nd	bharasi	bharathaḥ	bharatha
3rd	bharati	bharataḥ	bharanti

In Vedic also plur. 1st *-āmasi*, 2nd *-athana*.
Cf. *bhar-asi*, *-ati*, *-āmaḥ*, *-anti* with Lat. *leg-is*, *-it*, *-imus*, *-unt*.

Middle

1st	bhare	bharāvahe	bharāmahe
2nd	bharase	bharethe	bharadhve
3rd	bharate	bharete	bharante

bharase, *bharate*, *bharante* ~ Gr. φέρεαι, φέρεται, φέρονται.

Present Active Optative

1st	bhareyam	bhareva	bharema
2nd	bhareḥ	bharetam	bhareta
3rd	bharet	bharetām	bhareyuḥ

bhareḥ, *-et*, *-etam*, *-etām*, *-ema*, *-eta* = Gr. φέροις, φέροι, -οιτον, -οίτην, -οιμεν, -οιτε.

Middle

	Singular	Dual	Plural
1st	bhareya	bharevahi	bharemahi
2nd	bharethāḥ	bhareyāthām	bharedhvam
3rd	bhareta	bhareyātām	bhareran

Ved. plur. 3rd *bhareranta*. *bhareta*, *bharemahi* = Gr. φέροιτο, φεροίμεθα.

Present Active Imperative

1st	bharāṇi[20]	bharāva	bharāma
2nd	bhara	bharatam	bharata
3rd	bharatu	bharatām	bharantu

Also Vedic sing. 2nd and 3rd *-atāt* (Lat. *ag-itō*); plur. 2nd *-atana*. Cf. *bhara*, *bharata* with Gr. φέρε, φέρετε, Lat. *age*, *agite*. See §85.

Middle

1st	bharai	bharāvahai	bharāmahai
2nd	bharasva	bharethām	bharadhvam
3rd	bharatām	bharetām	bharantām

Imperfect Active

1st	abharam	abharāva	abharāma
2nd	abharaḥ	abharatam	abharata
3rd	abharat	abharatām	abharan

The characteristic sign of the imperfect is the augment *a-*; with the whole paradigm (with exception of the 1st dual) the Greek paradigm ἔφερον, -ες, -ε; -ετον, -έτην; -ομεν, -ετε, -ον can be compared. With regard to the endings Lat. *laudāba-m*, *-s*, *-t*, plur. 3rd *laudāba-nt* are also to be compared.

Middle

1st	abhare	abharāvahi	abharāmahi
2nd	abharathāḥ	abharethām	abharadhvam
3rd	abharata	abharetām	abharanta

abharata, *-āmahi*, *-anta* = Gr. ἐφέρετο, -όμεθα, -οντο.

[20] §20.

§85. Vedic still possesses a subjunctive, which is characterized in thematic verbs especially by the length of the thematic vowel, while the athematic verbs introduce a thematic vowel in the subjunctive (§§95, 99, etc.); this corresponds to the Greek situation, cf. subj. φέρ-ω-μεν (: indicative φέρ-ο-μεν), or ἴ-ο-μεν, younger ἴ-ω-μεν (: ind. ἴ-μεν). Subjunctives of thematic verbs have the following endings in the active: sing. 1st *-āni*, *-ā*, 2nd *-āsi*, *-āḥ*, 3rd *-āti*, *-āt*, dual 1st *-āva*, 2nd *āthaḥ*, 3rd *-ātaḥ*, plur. 1st *-āma*, 2nd *-ātha*, 3rd *-ān*. In the middle: sing. 1st *-ai*, 2nd *-āsai*, *-āse*, 3rd *-ātai*, *-āte*, dual 1st *-āvahai*, 2nd *-aithe*, 3rd *-aite*, plur. 1st *-āmahai*, 2nd *-ādhvai*, 3rd *-āntai*. The subjunctive still survives in the 1st persons of the imperative of the classical language (§84).

The injunctive of Vedic, to be defined formally as an augment form (imperfect, aorist) without augment, appears principally in prohibitive sentences; the nonprohibitive injunctive is tenseless and "nonreporting," i.e. it is used for the description of facts the hearer's knowledge of which is assumed. It still survives in the classical language in some imperative forms, which are distinguished from imperfect forms only by the lack of the augment (*bharatam* : *a-bharatam*); it is principally used in connection with the prohibitive negation *mā*, e.g. *mā kṛthāḥ* "do not do!" (: aor. *a-kṛthāḥ*).

(*b*) Athematic Verbs (Classes 2, 3, 5, 7, 8, 9)

§86. Common characteristics of all athematic verbs are:

The endings are added to the present stem or to the root without the intervening thematic vowel: thematic *bhar-a-ti*, athematic *as-ti*, *suno-ti*.

The root or the stem formation suffix is guṇated in the singular of the present active indicative and imperfect and in some additional forms; otherwise it has the fundamental-grade form: *e-mi* "I go": *i-maḥ* "we go," root *i-*. We speak here of strong and weak forms.

This gradation is an IE inheritance: cf. Gr. εἶ-μι: ἴ-μεν, δίδω-μι: δίδŏ-μεν, Lat. *es-t*: *s-unt*. Vedic manifests the reason for the gradation: the accent was on the ending in the nonsingular forms; *é-mi*, but *i-máḥ*; *ás-ti* "est": *s-ánti* "sunt."

The optative has the mood signs active *-yā-*, middle *-ī-* added to the weak stem.

The 2nd sing. active imperative has the ending *-dhi*, *-hi* (with few exceptions, §§ 100, 107).

Second Class[21]

§ 87. The endings are added directly to the root.

IE root present, type Gr. εἶ-μι, εἰ-μί, φη-μί, Lat. *es-t*, *vul-t*.

Paradigm *dviṣ-* "hate":

Active

Present Indicative

	Singular	Dual	Plural
1st	dveṣmi	dviṣvaḥ	dviṣmaḥ
2nd	dvekṣi	dviṣṭhaḥ	dviṣṭha
3rd	dveṣṭi	dviṣṭaḥ	dviṣanti

Optative

	Singular	Dual	Plural
1st	dviṣyām	dviṣyāva	dviṣyāma
2nd	dviṣyāḥ	dviṣyātam	dviṣyāta
3rd	dviṣyāt	dviṣyātām	dviṣyuḥ

Imperative

	Singular	Dual	Plural
1st	dveṣāṇi	dveṣāva	dveṣāma
2nd	dviḍḍhi	dviṣṭam	dviṣṭa
3rd	dveṣṭu	dviṣṭām	dviṣantu

Imperfect

	Singular	Dual	Plural
1st	adveṣam	adviṣva	adviṣma
2nd	adveṭ	adviṣṭam	adviṣṭa
3rd	adveṭ	adviṣṭām	adviṣan

[21] If the grammar is to be learned systematically, according to the presentation in this book, it is advisable to begin with a less complicated athematic class, perhaps with the fifth, and to become acquainted with the characteristics of the athematic verbs there.

Middle

Present Indicative

1st	dviṣe	dviṣvahe	dviṣmahe
2nd	dvikṣe	dviṣāthe	dviḍḍhve
3rd	dviṣṭe	dviṣāte	dviṣate

Optative

1st	dviṣīya	dviṣīvahi	dviṣīmahi
2nd	dviṣīthāḥ	dviṣīyāthām	dviṣīdhvam
3rd	dviṣīta	dviṣīyātām	dviṣīran

Imperative

1st	dveṣai	dveṣāvahai	dveṣāmahai
2nd	dvikṣva	dviṣāthām	dviḍḍhvam
3rd	dviṣṭām	dviṣātām	dviṣatām

Imperfect

1st	adviṣi	adviṣvahi	adviṣmahi
2nd	adviṣṭhāḥ	adviṣāthām	adviḍḍhvam
3rd	adviṣṭa	adviṣātām	adviṣata

Various combinatory sound laws cause the difficulties of this paradigm (see concerning this p. 75, note 21): thus *-ṣ+s-* becomes **-ṭṣ-* under conditions not yet completely explained (cf. **a-dveṣ-s* > *adveṭ* impf. 2nd sing.), but also *-kṣ-* (*dvekṣi* < *dveṣ+si*; also *dvikṣe*, *dvikṣva*); *-ṣ+t-* becomes *-ṣṭ-* (§19): *dveṣ-ṭi*, *dviṣ-ṭe*, etc.; *-ṣ+d(h)-* resulted in *ḍḍ(h)* after passing through a stage of **ẓḍ(h)*: *dviṣ+dhi* > *dviḍḍhi*. See further *dviḍḍhve*, *(a)dviḍḍhvam*.

Sound laws also determine the peculiarities of additional verbs of this class:

duh- "milk": *dohmi*, *dhokṣi* (§30, 2), *dogdhi* (§30, 1), plural *duhmaḥ*, *dugdha*, *duhanti*; middle *duhe*, *dhukṣe*, *dugdhe*, etc.

lih- "lick": *lehmi*, *lekṣi*, *leḍhi*, *lihmaḥ*, *līḍha*, *lihanti*, etc.

leḍhi for *leh-* < **-źh-* + ending *-ti*, §30, 1.

§88. The conjugation of the root *as-* "be" shows peculiarities:

Indicative

	Singular	Dual	Plural
1st	asmi	svaḥ	smaḥ
2nd	asi	sthaḥ	stha
3rd	asti	staḥ	santi

asmi = Gr. εἰμί, Goth. *im*; *asi* = Gr. εἶ, Lat. *es*, Goth. *is*; *asti* = Gr. ἐστί, Lat. *est*, Goth. *ist*; *santi* = Lat. *sunt*, Goth. *sind*.

Optative

1st	syām	syāva	syāma
2nd	syāḥ	syātam	syāta
3rd	syāt	syātām	syuḥ

syām, *syāḥ*, *syāt*—Old Latin *siem*, *siēs*, *siet*, later *sim*, etc.

Imperative

1st	asāni	asāva	asāma
2nd	edhi	stam	sta
3rd	astu	stām	santu

edhi from **azdhi*, *as* + *dhi*, cf. § 14.

Imperfect

1st	āsam	āsva	āsma
2nd	āsīḥ	āstam	āsta
3rd	āsīt	āstām	āsan

āsam, *āstam*, *āstām*, *āsma*, *āsta* = Gr. ἦα, ἦστον, ἤστην, ἦμεν, ἦστε.

§ 89. *i*- "go": pres. act. ind. sing. *emi*, *eṣi*, *eti*, plur. *imaḥ*, *itha*, *yanti*; imperative *ay-āni*, *ihi*, *etu*, plur. *ayāma*, *ita*, *yantu*; imperfect *āyam*, *aiḥ*, *ait*, plur. *aima*, *aita*, *āyan*; optative *iyām*, *iyāḥ*, etc.

Middle: Cf. *adhīte* 3rd sing. "he learns" (*adhi-i-te*).

Cf. the forms of the pres. ind. with Gr. εἶμι, εἶ, εἶσι, ἴμεν; imper. *ihi*, *ita* = Gr. ἴθι, ἴτε; impf. *āyam*, *aima* < *a*- (augment) + **ai*- (§ 14), = Gr. ᾖ-α, ᾖμεν.

§90. *an-* "breathe," *jakṣ-* "eat," *rud-* "cry," *śvas-* "breathe," *svap-* "sleep" all add endings beginning with a consonant (except with *y-*) to stems in *-i-*: *an-i-ti*, *rud-i-maḥ*. The 2nd and 3rd person sing. imperfect forms end in *-aḥ*, *-at* or in *-īḥ*, *-īt*.

§91. *brū-* "speak" has a stem *bravī-* in the strong (guṇated) forms (§86): *bravīmi*, *bravīṣi*, *bravīti*, plur. *brūmaḥ*, *brūtha*, *bruvanti*, etc.

stu- "praise" has the strong stems *stau-* and *stavī-*: *stauti*, *stavīti*: *stumaḥ*.

§92. The deponent *śī-* "lie" shows guṇa (*śe-*) in the whole present and imperfect: 3rd sing. *śete*: 1st plur. *śemahe*, etc. To be especially noted are: 3rd plur. pres. ind. *śerate*, imperative *śeratām*, imperfect *aśerata*.

śete ~ Gr. κεῖται; *śemahe* ~ κείμεθα.

§93. *śās-* "order" has *śāsati* as 3rd plur. in the indicative, *śāsatu* in the imperative, *aśāsuḥ* in the imperfect, but also shows a weak stem form *śiṣ-*: opt. *śiṣ-yām*, p.p.p. *śiṣ-ṭa-*.

-ati, *-atu* from **-n̥ti*, **-n̥tu* (§8); *śiṣ-* from **k̑əs-*, cf. §§11, 25.

vaś- "want" shows *uś-* in the weak forms: 1st sing. *vaśmi*, 3rd plur. *uś-anti*.

han- "kill" has *ha-* as its weak root form before endings beginning with a consonant (but *han-* before *-vaḥ*, *-maḥ*); *ghn-* before endings beginning with a vowel. The 2nd sing. imperative is *jahi*. Present *hanmi*, *haṁsi*, *hanti*, *hanvaḥ*, *hathaḥ*, *hataḥ*, *hanmaḥ*, *hatha*, *ghnanti*, etc.

Cf. §27.

§94. Some verbs of class 2 show no gradation (§86); thus *yā-* "go" always has guṇa grade (pres. act. ind. *yāmi*, *yāsi*, *yāti*, plur. *yāmaḥ*, *yātha*, *yānti*, imperf. *a-yā-m*, etc.), likewise the deponent *ās-* "sit" (3rd person sing. *ās-te*, plur. *ās-ate*). Deponents like *sū-* "bear," *īś-* "be master of" always show the fundamental grade, never guṇa (3rd sing. mid. *sū-te*, *īṣ-ṭe*); etc.

§95. A peculiarity of Vedic for this class is, above all, the formation of the subjunctive. It is formed by the introduction of a thematic vowel, according to §85. Cf. sing. 2nd *áy-a-si*, *áy-aḥ* (: ind. *é-ṣi*) from *i-* "go," §89; sing. 3rd *ás-a-ti*, *ás-a-t* (: ind. *ás-ti*), root *as-*, §88, etc. Further, from *as-* "be," 2nd and 3rd sing. imperf. *āḥ* (<*ās-s*, **ās-t*; =Dor. Gr. ἦς 3rd sing.); opt. 2nd plur. *syāta-na*. From *brū-* (§91) 2nd sing. imper. *brū-tāt* (cf. §84), 2nd plur. *bravītana*. *śī-* (§92) has in Ved. 3rd sing. ind. *śáy-e*, 3rd plur. *śé-re*; 3rd sing. impf. *áśayat*, 3rd plur. *áśeran*. *śās-* (§93): 2nd plur. imper. *śāstána*. Often 1st plur. *-masi* beside *-maḥ*; etc.

Third Class

§96. The root is reduplicated; the following rules apply to the reduplication:

A. Aspirates are reduplicated by the corresponding unaspirated sounds, velars always by their palatals: thus *dh-* by *d-*; *bh-* by *b-*; *k-*, *kh-* by *c-*; *g-*, *gh-*, and also *h-* by *j-*.

B. Consonant groups are reduplicated by the first consonant (or by its representative, according to A above); only the combination sibilant+stop is reduplicated by means of the second sound (or its representative, according to A).

C. The rules given above also apply to other grammatical cases in which reduplication is used (§121). For the reduplicated presents of class 3 it should be noted that the short root vowel enters into the reduplication syllable: thus *hu-* "sacrifice": *ju-hu-maḥ* "we sacrifice"; *bhī-* "fear": *bi-bhī-*; *dhā-* "place": *dadhā-*; but note *bhṛ-* "bear": *bi-bhar-ti*, *bi-bhṛ-maḥ*; *mā-* "measure" (deponent): *mi-mī-te* 3rd sing., *mi-mate* 3rd plur.

This is an IE reduplicating present type; cf. Gr. δί-δω-μι, ἵ-στᾱ-μι, πίμ-πλη-μι from the roots δω-, στᾱ-, πλη-.

§97. Paradigm *hu*-[22] "sacrifice":

Active

Present Indicative

	Singular	Dual	Plural
1st	juhomi	juhuvaḥ	juhumaḥ
2nd	juhoṣi	juhuthaḥ	juhutha
3rd	juhoti	juhutaḥ	juhvati[23]

Optative

1st	juhuyām	juhuyāva	juhuyāma
2nd	juhuyāḥ	juhuyātam	juhuyāta
3rd	juhuyāt	juhuyātām	juhuyuḥ

Imperative

1st	juhavāni[24]	juhavāva	juhavāma
2nd	juhudhi	juhutam	juhuta
3rd	juhotu	juhutām	juhvatu

Imperfect

1st	ajuhavam[24]	ajuhuva	ajuhuma
2nd	ajuhoḥ	ajuhutam	ajuhuta
3rd	ajuhot	ajuhutām	ajuhavuḥ

Middle

Present Indicative

1st	juhve[25]	juhuvahe	juhumahe
2nd	juhuṣe	juhvāthe	juhudhve
3rd	juhute	juhvāte	juhvate

[22] Guṇated stem (§86) *ju-ho-*, weak stem *ju-hu-*; for the reduplication see §96 A, C.

[23] *-ati*, etc. from **-n̥ti* (§8): *bhara-nti*, etc.

[24] *juhav-āni*, *a-juhav-am*, etc. show the prevocalic form of the stem *juho-*, since *-o-* goes back to **-ău-* (§14); but the 1st person sing. impf. of *dhā-*, *hā-* (§§98, 99) is conjugated *a-dadhā-m*, *a-jahā-m*, etc.

[25] From **juhu-e*, *juhu-īya*, etc.

Optative

	Singular	Dual	Plural
1st	juhvīya[25]	juhvīvahi	juhvīmahi
etc.			

Imperative

1st	juhavai	juhavāvahai	juhavāmahai
2nd	juhuṣva	juhvāthām	juhudhvam
3rd	juhutām	juhvātām	juhvatām

Imperfect

1st	ajuhvi	ajuhuvahi	ajuhumahi
2nd	ajuhuthāḥ	ajuhvāthām	ajuhudhvam
3rd	ajuhuta	ajuhvātām	ajuhvata

§98. *dhā-* "put, place" and the similarly inflected *dā-* "give" deviate in part from §97, above all because of their weak stem form *da-dh-*, *da-d*, but also because of phonetic differences, concerning which the reader should refer especially to §30, 2 for *dhā-*.

Active Indicative

	Singular	Dual	Plural
1st	dadhāmi	dadhvaḥ	dadhmaḥ
2nd	dadhāsi	dhatthaḥ	dhattha
3rd	dadhāti	dhattaḥ	dadhati

Optative

1st	dadhyām	dadhyāva	dadhyāma
etc.			

Imperative

1st	dadhāni	dadhāva	dadhāma
2nd	dhehi	dhattam	dhatta
3rd	dadhātu	dhattām	dadhatu

Imperfect

	Singular	Dual	Plural
1st	adadhām	adadhva	adadhma
2nd	adadhāḥ	adhattam	adhatta
3rd	adadhāt	adhattām	adadhuḥ

Middle Indicative: *dadhe*, *dhatse*, *dhatte*, etc.

Beside *dhehí* "put!", *dehí* "give!" we have *da-d-dhí* in Ved.; the first forms go back to dissimilated **d(h)azdhí* (Av. *dazdī*), with *-e-* < *-az-* (§14); cf. K. Hoffmann, *Münchener Stud. z. Sprachwiss.*, Vol. 8 (1956), p. 21. *dádhāmi*, *dádhāti*, *dadhmáḥ* (Ved. accentuation: see §86) ~ Gr. τίθημι, τίθησι, τίθĕμεν.

§99. *hā-* "leave" has *jahi-* and *jahī-* as a weak stem before endings beginning with a consonant, *jah-* before endings beginning with a vowel or with *y-*: present ind. *jahāmi*, *jahāsi*, *jahāti*, plur. *jahimāḥ* (*jahīmaḥ*), *jahitha* (*jahītha*), *jahati*, opt. *jahyām*, etc.

Vedic: Subjunctives like sg. 1st *bibhar-āṇi* 3rd *bibhar-a-t* (: ind. *bi-bhar-mi*, *-ti*) according to §§85, 95; 1st plur. active *-masi*; 3rd sing. mid. *-e*; 2nd sing. imper. *-tāt*, etc.

Fifth Class

§100. The present stems of this class are formed by addition of strong *-no-*, weak *-nu-* (*-nv-*) to the root.

The Old Ind. stem sign *-no-*/*-nu-* is IE **-neu-*/**-nu-*; in Greek -νεύω, -νέω and, above all, -νῡ-μι appear for **-neu-mi* (: Old Ind. *-no-mi*); cf. δείκ-νῡ-μι, plur. δείκ-νῠ-μεν (: Old Ind. *-nu-maḥ*).

Concerning the ultimate origin of this present type see below, §102.

Paradigm *su-* "press grapes":

Active

Present Indicative

	Singular	Dual	Plural
1st	sunomi	sunuvaḥ	sunumaḥ
2nd	sunoṣi	sunuthaḥ	sunutha
3rd	sunoti	sunutaḥ	sunvanti

Optative

	Singular	Dual	Plural
1st	sunuyām	sunuyāva	sunuyāma
etc.			

Imperative

1st	sunavāni	sunavāva	sunavāma
2nd	sunu	sunutam	sunuta
3rd	sunotu	sunutām	sunvantu

Imperfect

1st	asunavam	asunuva	asunuma
2nd	asunoḥ	asunutam	asunuta
3rd	asunot	asunutām	asunvan

Middle

Present Indicative

1st	sunve	sunuvahe	sunumahe
2nd	sunuṣe	sunvāthe	sunudhve
3rd	sunute	sunvāte	sunvate

Optative

1st	sunvīya	sunvīvahi	sunvīmahi
etc.			

Imperative

1st	sunavai	sunavāvahai	sunavāmahai
2nd	sunuṣva	sunvāthām	sunudhvam
3rd	sunutām	sunvātām	sunvatām

Imperfect

1st	asunvi	asunuvahi	asunumahi
2nd	asunuthāḥ	asunvāthām	asunudhvam
3rd	asunuta	asunvātām	asunvata

u can also be lacking before endings which begin with *v* or *m*: *sunvaḥ*, *sunmaḥ* beside *sunuvaḥ*, *sunumaḥ*; *sunvahe*, *asunva*, *asunvahi*, *asunma*, *asunmahi*.

This possibility does not apply to roots ending in a consonant, such as *āp*- "obtain": here only *āpnuvaḥ*, *āpnumaḥ*, etc. are admissible; forms which show *-nv-* with roots ending in a vowel are also conjugated like the 3rd plur. act.: *āpnuvanti* (cf. *sun-v-anti*). These roots have the ending *-hi* in the 2nd sing. imper. (*āp-nu-hi* "obtain!" as opposed to *sunu*).

In Vedic *-hi*, *-dhi* also occur with roots ending in a vowel: *ci-nu-hí*, *śṛ-ṇu-dhí* (§101). Vedic also shows for this class, among others, the additional forms: 1st plur. active *-masi*, 3rd sing. mid. *-e*, 3rd plur. *-i-re* (*su-nv-iré*); imper. 2nd sing. *-tāt*, 2nd plur. *-tana*; subjunctive forms (according to §§85, 95), like 2nd sing. *śṛ-ṇáv-aḥ*, 3rd *śṛṇávat*, *sunávat* (: ind. *śṛṇóṣi*, *-óti*); etc.

§101. *śru*- "hear" shows the stems: strong *śṛ-ṇo-*, weak *śṛ-ṇu-*, *śṛṇv-*.

Cf. in addition §102!

Seventh Class

§102. This class forms the present stem by addition of a *-na-* (*-n-* in the weak forms) between the vowel and the final consonant of the root (infixing class). Thus the 1st sing. pres. act. ind. of the root *yuj*- "harness" is *yu-na-j-mi*, the 1st plur. *yu-ñ-j-maḥ*.[26]

IE **i̯u-ne-g-mi* (: root *i̯ug*-), certainly a very ancient type: cf. cases outside Indo-Iranian, like Gr. βυνέω "fill," probably for *βυ-νε-σ-μι, and the later formation Lat. *iu-n-g-ō*. The nasal-infixing principle is also to be referred to for the explanation of the other nasal classes, such as the Old Ind. 5th (§100) and 9th (§106) classes; in connection with this we compare, with their pre-Old Indic values:

[26] *-ñ-* from **-n-* before palatal *-j-*.

Cl. 7, act. 1st sg. *yu-na-j-mi*, 1st pl. *yu-ñ-j-maḥ*, p.p.p. *yuk-ta-*, root *yug-*.

Cl. 5, act. 1st sg. **śṛ-ṇa-u-mi* > *śṛ-ṇo-mi* (§14), 1st pl. *śṛ-ṇ-u-maḥ*, p.p.p. *śru-ta-*, root *śru-* (§101);

Cl. 9, act. 1st sg. **pu-na-ə-mi* > *punāmi* "purify," 1st pl. **pu-n-ə-maḥ* > *punīmaḥ*, p.p.p. **puə-ta-* > *pūta-*, root *pū-* (see §§11, 37).

§103. Paradigm *rudh-* "obstruct" (*ru-ṇa-dh-/ru-n-dh-*); the application of §30, 1 (*-dh-t-* > *-ddh-*) is to be noted here.

Active

Present Indicative

	Singular	Dual	Plural
1st	ruṇadhmi	rundhvaḥ	rundhmaḥ
2nd	ruṇatsi	runddhaḥ	runddha
3rd	ruṇaddhi	runddhaḥ	rundhanti

Optative

1st	rundhyām	rundhyāva	rundhyāma
etc.			

Imperative

1st	ruṇadhāni	ruṇadhāva	ruṇadhāma
2nd	runddhi	runddham	runddha
3rd	ruṇaddhu	runddhām	rundhantu

Imperfect

1st	aruṇadham	arundhva	arundhma
2nd	aruṇat	arunddham	arunddha
3rd	aruṇat	arunddhām	arundhan

Middle

Present Indicative

1st	rundhe	rundhvahe	rundhmahe
2nd	runtse	rundhāthe	runddhve
3rd	runddhe	rundhāte	rundhate

Optative

	Singular	Dual	Plural
1st	rundhīya	rundhīvahi	rundhīmahi
etc.			

Imperative

1st	ruṇadhai	ruṇadhāvahai	ruṇadhāmahai
2nd	runtsva	rundhāthām	runddhvam
3rd	runddhām	rundhātām	rundhatām

Imperfect

1st	arundhi	arundhvahi	arundhmahi
2nd	arunddhāḥ	arundhāthām	arunddhvam
3rd	arunddha	arundhātām	arundhata

From Vedic cf. especially subjunctive forms like 3rd sing. *yunáj-a-t* (: ind. *yunák-ti*); 3rd sing. mid. *-e* beside *-te*.

Eighth Class

§104. Most roots of this class end in *-n*: *tan-* "stretch," *man-* "think" (dep.), *san-* "win," *kṣan-* "hurt," etc. The stem-formation suffix is *-o-*, in the weak forms *-u-*: *tan-o-mi*, *tan-u-maḥ* "I stretch, we stretch." The conjugation is exactly the same as that of *sunomi*: *sunumaḥ*, that is, that of the Old Ind. 5th class (§100).

From a historical point of view the establishment of the "8th class" has no justification, for *tanomi* is not to be analyzed into *tan-o-mi*, as the Indians must have thought, but belongs, like **tn̥-neu-mi* (§8), to **tn̥-*, the weak grade of *tan-*, just as *su-no-mi* belongs to the weak-grade root form *su-*; thus verbs of the *neu-* class, §100, are under consideration here. Cf. also §105.

§105. The strong stem of the frequent verb of this class *kr̥-* "do, make" is *karo-*; the weak stem is *kuru-*, before *-m-*, *-y-*, and *-v-* only *kur-*: pres. sing. *karomi*, *karoṣi*, *karoti*, dual *kurvaḥ*, *kuruthaḥ*, *kurutaḥ*, plural *kurmaḥ*, *kurutha*, *kurvanti*, optative *kuryām*, etc.

karoti is not to be separated from an older attested present formation of this root, Ved. *kṛ-ṇó-ti* (thus 5th class). For the many attempts at explanation, see the lit. in Thumb–Hauschild, *Handbuch des Sanskrit*, Vol. 1, 2 (1959), pp. 267 ff., and W. P. Schmid, *Indogermanische Forschungen*, Vol. 65 (1960), pp. 235 ff.

Ninth Class

§106. The sign for the present is *-nā-* in the strong stem, *-nī-* in the weak stem, *-n-* before endings beginning with a vowel.

Old Ind. *-nā-mi*, *-nī-maḥ*, *-n-anti* < IE **-nā-mi*, **-nə-mes*, **-n̥ə̯-enti*; Gr. δάμ-νη-μι, δάμ-νᾰ-μεν. The ultimate origin of this present formation is probably infixation (§102) in seṭ-roots (§37), whose final *-ə* appeared after the infix. The present of **peu̯ə-* "purify" (> Old Ind. *pavī̆-tár-* m. "purifier," *pavi-tum* inf.) was **pu-ne-ə-ti* (> Old Ind. *punāti*), just as, for **i̯eug-* "harness," the present was **i̯u-ne-g-ti* (> Old Ind. *yunakti*).

Paradigm *krī-* "buy":

Active

Present Indicative

	Singular	Dual	Plural
1st	krīṇāmi[27]	krīṇīvaḥ	krīṇīmaḥ
2nd	krīṇāsi	krīṇīthaḥ	krīṇītha
3rd	krīṇāti	krīṇītaḥ	krīṇanti

Optative

1st	krīṇīyām	krīṇīyāva	krīṇīyāma
etc.			

Imperative

1st	krīṇāni	krīṇāva	krīṇāma
2nd	krīṇīhi	krīṇītam	krīṇīta
3rd	krīṇātu	krīṇītām	krīṇantu

[27] -ṇ- according to §20.

Imperfect

	Singular	Dual	Plural
1st	akrīṇām	akrīṇīva	akrīṇīma
2nd	akrīṇāḥ	akrīṇītam	akrīṇīta
3rd	akrīṇāt	akrīṇītām	akrīṇan

Middle

Present Indicative

1st	krīṇe	krīṇīvahe	krīṇīmahe
2nd	krīṇīṣe	krīṇāthe	krīṇīdhve
3rd	krīṇīte	krīṇāte	krīṇate

Optative

1st	krīṇīya	krīṇīvahi	krīṇīmahi
etc.			

Imperative

1st	krīṇai	krīṇāvahai	krīṇāmahai
2nd	krīṇīṣva	krīṇāthām	krīṇīdhvam
3rd	krīṇītām	krīṇātām	krīṇatām

Imperfect

1st	akrīṇi	akrīṇīvahi	akrīṇīmahi
2nd	akrīṇīthāḥ	akrīṇāthām	akrīṇīdhvam
3rd	akrīṇīta	akrīṇātām	akrīṇata

§107. Roots of this class which end in a consonant (like *aś-* "eat," *grah-* "seize") form the 2nd sing. imper. act. in *-āna*: *aśāna* "eat!," *gṛhāṇa* "seize!" (as opposed to *krīṇīhi*).

§108. *grah-* "seize," *bandh-* "bind," *stambh-* "prop," *jñā-* "know" form *gṛhṇāmi*, *badhnāmi*, *stabhnāmi*, *jānāmi*.

These are the usual zero grades with the presents of the 9th cl.: *-r̥-* to *-ra-*, *-a-* < **-n̥-* (§8) to *-an-*, *jā-* < **ǵn̥ə-* (§9) to *jñā-* < **ǵnō-*. More archaic than the latter is the type of zero grade in *-ə* (like **puə-* > *pū-*), whose *-ə*, according to §106, does not appear before the infix. The following rule relates to them:

§109. Roots in *-ū*, like *pū-* "purify," *lū-* "cut," show short *-u-* before *-nā-/-n(ī)-*: *punāmi, lunāmi.*

Some subjunctive forms of this class appear in Vedic, for example, act. 2nd sing. *gṛbhṇā́ḥ*, 1st plur. *junā́ma*, mid. 1st dual *krīṇāvahai*; forms with the following special endings also appear: act. 1st plur. *-masi*, 2nd plur. *-thana*, mid. 3rd sing. *-e*, imper. act. 2nd sing. *-tāt*, plur. *-tana*.

The Nonpresent Forms

§110. Like the present stems (§§83–109), the aorist stems, perfect stems, and future stems, as well as additional derivative forms, are formed directly from the root.

1. Aorists

In classical Sanskrit the aorist is used as a past tense beside imperfect and perfect, without distinction. Its forms thus retreat more and more before those of the other two preterites. Vedic, however, still shows a full array of aorist forms, augmented and augmentless, and even has subjunctives, optatives, imperatives of aorists. Concerning aorist injunctives, which still play a role in Sanskrit, see above, §85.

(*a*) asigmatic aorists

§111. The root aorist is formed by means of the augment (*a-*), the pure root, and athematic endings.

Paradigms *dā-* "give," *bhū-* "be, become."

	Singular		Dual		Plural	
1st	adām	abhūvam	adāva	abhūva	adāma	abhūma
2nd	adāḥ	abhūḥ	adātam	abhūtam	adāta	abhūta
3rd	adāt	abhūt	adātām	abhūtām	aduḥ	abhūvan

Cf. the Gr. root aorists like ἔφῡν, ἔστην, ἔβην, ἔ-θε-μεν.

§112. The thematic aorist is equal to an imperfect of the 6th class (§83). Thus the imperfects from the roots *sic-*, *sad-*, *gam-*, *lip-*—according to the present stem—are *asiñcam*, *asīdam*, *agaccham*, *alimpam*, but the aorists are *asicam*, *asadam*, *agamam*, *alipam*. Inflection like *abharam* (§84), etc.

Cf. Gr. aorists like ἔλιπον, ἔφυγον, for the presents λείπω, φεύγω.

§113. The reduplicating aorist is likewise inflected thematically. The vowel of the reduplication syllable is usually quantitatively different from that of the root syllable; with roots with medial *-a-* and in *-ā*, *-ṝ*, *-ṛ* it is usually *-i-*, *-ī-*. Cf. for *cur-* 10 "steal": *a-cū-cur-am*; for *gaṇ-* 10 "compute": *a-jī-gaṇam*; for *nī-* 1 causative (§129): *anīnayam*; for *sthā-* 1 causative (*sthāpayati*, §129): *atiṣṭhipam*; for *naś-* 4 "get lost": *aneśam*; for *pat-* 1 "fly": *apaptam*; for *vac-* 2 "speak": *avocam*; etc.

Cf. Gr. reduplicating thematic aorists like ἔ-πε-φν-ον.

(*b*) sigmatic aorists

§114. The athematic *s*-aorist. The augmented root shows vṛddhi (§35) in the active, fundamental grade in the middle, guṇa with roots in final *-ĭ*, *-ŭ*; to the root is added *-s-* (or *-ṣ-* according to §25) with athematic endings.

Paradigms: *nī-* 1 "lead" (aorist stem act. *a-nai-ṣ-*, mid. *a-ne-ṣ-* [guṇa]); *yuj-* 7 "bind, harness" (*a-yauk-ṣ-*, *a-yuk-ṣ-*):

	Active		Middle	
	Singular			
1st	anaiṣam	ayaukṣam	aneṣi	ayukṣi
2nd	anaiṣīḥ	ayaukṣīḥ	aneṣṭhāḥ	ayukthāḥ
3rd	anaiṣīt	ayaukṣīt	aneṣṭa	ayukta
	Dual			
1st	anaiṣva	ayaukṣva	aneṣvahi	ayukṣvahi
2nd	anaiṣṭam	ayauktam	aneṣāthām	ayukṣāthām
3rd	anaiṣṭām	ayauktām	aneṣātām	ayukṣātām

	Active		Middle	
		Plural		
1st	anaiṣma	ayaukṣma	aneṣmahi	ayukṣmahi
2nd	anaiṣṭa	ayaukta	aneḍhvam	ayugdhvam
3rd	anaiṣuḥ	ayaukṣuḥ	aneṣata	ayukṣata

The peculiarities of these paradigms are explained by phonetic processes: for example, *-s-* in the group **-k-s-t-* is eliminated; therefore we have *a-yauk-ta* as opposed to *a-yauk-ṣ-ma*; *-ṣ-* before *d*° becomes voiced (**ẓ*) and disappears by cerebralization: *aneḍhvam* for *a-neṣ + dhvam*. For *rudh-* "obstruct," on the other hand, the active plural forms, for example, are: 1st *a-raut-s-ma* (assimilation *-dh-s-* > *-ts-*), 2nd *arauddha* (**a-raudh- + ta*, §30, 1), 3rd *arautsuḥ*.

Compare the Gr. *s*-aorists like ἔδειξα, ἔζευξα, ἔγραψα, and the Lat. perfects of *s*-aorist origin like *vēxī*, *dīxī*, *dūxī*.

§115. The *iṣ*-aorist. *-iṣ-* is added to the augmented root (guṇated, with final vowel vṛddhied in the active). Endings as in §114. Cf. *lū-* 9 "cut off": *a-lāv-iṣ-am*, *alāvīḥ*, *alāvīt*, plur. *alāviṣma*, *alāviṣṭa*, *alāviṣuḥ*; middle *alaviṣi*, *alaviṣṭhāḥ*, *alaviṣṭa*, etc.; *budh-* 1 "awaken": *abodhiṣam*, *abodhiṣi*; *pū-* 9 "purify": *apāviṣam*, *apaviṣi*; *grah-* 9 "seize": *agrahīṣam* (*-ī-*).

Rather frequent in the older language, but only a few examples left in classical Sanskrit. Since this aorist generally belongs to seṭ-roots (§37), *-iṣ-* will chiefly go back to root-final *-ə + s-*; cf. also Gr. forms like ἐδάμασσα, ἐκρέμασσα.

§116. The *siṣ*-aorist. This rare formation is found only with some roots in *-ā*, diphthongs, and *-am*. It is solely active. *-siṣ-* is added athematically to the guṇated root bearing the augment; cf. *yā-* 2 "go": *ayāsiṣam*; *ram-* 1 "enjoy oneself": *araṁsiṣam*.

§117. The *sa*-aorist. *-sa* -is joined to the augmented weak-grade root. The inflection is thus thematic, and this aorist is conjugated in the active like *abharam* (§84); in the middle there are some deviations. The *sa*-aorist of *diś*- 6 "show" is in the active *adikṣam* (§24), *-aḥ*, *-at*, etc., in the middle *adikṣi*, *adikṣathāḥ*, *adikṣata*, *adikṣāvahi*, *adikṣāthām*, *adikṣātām*, *adikṣāmahi*, *adikṣadhvam*, *adikṣanta*.

§118. A rare modal form related to the *s*-aorist, which has approximately the function of the optative, is called the precative; it is formed in the active by the addition of *-yās-* with athematic endings to the weak root form. *budh-* 1 "awaken" has the following paradigm:

	Singular	Dual	Plural
1st	budhyāsam	budhyāsva	budhyāsma
2nd	budhyāḥ	budhyāstam	budhyāsta
3rd	budhyāt	budhyāstām	budhyāsuḥ

Historical explanation by T. Burrow, *Festschrift F. Weller* (1954), pp. 35 ff., *Indo-Iranian Journal*, Vol. 1 (1957), pp. 61 ff.

2. Future

§119. To the root, almost always guṇated, is added the thematic suffix *-sya-* (or *-ṣya-* according to §25), with some roots *-iṣya-*. Inflection like §84. Cf. *dā-* "give": *dāsyāmi*, *dāsyasi*, *dāsyati*, etc., middle *dāsye*, *dāsyase*, *dāsyate*; *kṛ-* "make": *kar-i-ṣyāmi*, mid. *kariṣye*.

Additional examples: *nī-* "lead," *neṣyāmi*; *labh-* "take," *lapsyāmi*; *vas-* "dwell," *vatsyāmi* (*-ss-* > *-ts-*); *dṛś-* "see," *drakṣyāmi*; *grah-* "seize," *grahīṣyāmi*; *sad-* "sit," *sīdiṣyāmi*; verbs of the 10th class and causatives (§§83, 129) keep *-ay-* and add *-iṣya-*: *pat-*, causative *pātayati*: *pātayiṣyāmi*.

The rare conditional is formally an "imperfect" of the future: *adāsyam* "I would give, would have given, should have given."

§120. A noun of agent in *-tṛ-* (*dā-tṛ-* "giver": *dā-*) forms a periphrastic future with the verb "to be" (*as-*, §88): *dātāsmi* "I shall give" < *dātā asmi*. The third persons are without verbal form.

Active

	Singular	Dual	Plural
1st	dātāsmi	dātāsvaḥ	dātāsmaḥ
2nd	dātāsi	dātāsthaḥ	dātāstha
3rd	dātā	dātārau	dātāraḥ

Middle

	Singular	Dual	Plural
1st	dātāhe	dātāsvahe	dātāsmahe
2nd	dātāse	dātāsāthe	dātādhve
3rd	dātā	dātārau	dātāraḥ

3. Perfect

§121. The stem of the perfect is formed from the root by reduplication; this follows for the most part the rules given in §96, but the reduplication vowel for roots in *-ṛ*, *-ṝ* and diphthongs is *-a-*. Initial *a-*, *ā-* become *ā-* in the perfect stem (*ad-* "eat": perf. *ād-a*, *āp-* "obtain": *āpa*); initial *ṛ-* and *a-* before several consonants have the reduplication syllable *ān-*: *ṛdh-* "develop," perfect stem *ān-ṛdh-*, *añj-* "besmear," *ānañj-*. Roots beginning with *i-*, *u-* are reduplicated by *iy-*, *uv-*, which are contracted with the root vowel in the weak forms, giving *ī-*, *ū-* (§122): *iṣ-* "wish," *iy-eṣ-a*, *īṣ-uḥ*; *uṣ-* "burn," *uvoṣa*, *ūṣuḥ*; roots with *ya*, *va* are reduplicated by *i*, *u*; the weak-grade form in the weak stem (§122), *i*, *u*, is combined with these reduplications, giving *ī*, *ū*: *yaj-* "sacrifice," *i-yāj-a*, *īj-uḥ*; *vac-* "speak," *uvāca*, *ūcuḥ*.

§122. The root is generally guṇated (strong) in the active singular, but is of weak grade (weak) in the remaining forms. Roots with medial *-a-* have *-a-* or *-ā-* in the 1st sing. act., always *-ā-* in the 3rd sing. Likewise, roots in *-i*, *-ī*, *-u*, *-ū*, *-ṛ*, *-ṝ* have vṛddhi optionally in the 1st sing. act. but always have vṛddhi in the 3rd sing. Roots which begin and end with a consonant and whose vowel is long by nature or by position (*jīv-*, *nind-*) show no gradation.

§ 123. Moreover, the perfect shows special endings, which are set off by hyphens in the first of the following paradigms.

(*a*) Paradigm *tud-* "push" (strong perfect stem *tu-tod-*, weak stem *tu-tud-*):

Active

	Singular	Dual	Plural
1st	tutod-a	tutud-i-va	tutud-i-ma
2nd	tutod-i-tha	tutud-athuḥ	tutud-a
3rd	tutod-a	tutud-atuḥ	tutud-uḥ

Middle

1st	tutud-e	tutud-i-vahe	tutud-i-mahe
2nd	tutud-i-ṣe	tutud-āthe	tutud-i-dhve
3rd	tutud-e	tutud-āte	tutud-ire

(*b*) Paradigm *kṛ-* "do"; (*c*) *gam-* "go"; (*d*) *jīv-* "live."

These paradigms, given only in the active, show that the "connecting vowel" *-i-* standing before some endings can be lacking (*b*) or can be used optionally (*c*); they show the lengthening of the medial *-a-* of *gam-* (weak form *gm-*) and of the guṇa form of *kṛ-* (*kar-*) in the 3rd person singular, optionally in the 1st person singular (§ 122), as well as the lack of gradation in *jīv-* (§ 122).

Singular

1st	cakara, cakāra	jagama, jagāma	jijīva
2nd	cakartha	jagantha, jagamitha	jijīvitha
3rd	cakāra	jagāma	jijīva

Dual

1st	cakṛva	jagmiva	jijīviva
2nd	cakrathuḥ	jagmathuḥ	jijīvathuḥ
3rd	cakratuḥ	jagmatuḥ	jijīvatuḥ

Plural

1st	cakṛma	jagmima	jijīvima
2nd	cakra	jagma	jijīva
3rd	cakruḥ	jagmuḥ	jijīvuḥ

The Vedic language deviates from this, above all, in the following details: *-rire* also appears in the 3rd plur. mid. (*vi-vid-rire*); the "connecting vowel" is distributed differently; many reduplications contradict the classical rules (*sa-sū-*, root *sū-* "bear"; lengthened *vā-vṛt-*, root *vṛt-* "roll"); we find subjunctives, optatives, imperatives of the perfect stem, as well as an augmented pluperfect. The position of the Vedic accent explains why the root has full grade only in the sing. act., for the accent falls upon the ending in all other forms. Cf. act. 1st sing. *tutóda*, but du. *tutudivá*, pl. *tutudimá*, sing. mid. *tutudé*.

Compare the reduplicated perfects like Gr. δέδορκα, λέλοιπα, Lat. *memordī/momordī*, *tetulī*, *tutudī*; Old Ind. *cakar-a*, cf. Gr. δέδορκ-α, *-tha* = Gr. οἶσ-θα (§126), *-a* = Gr. -ε. The length of medial *-ā-* in the 3rd sg. act. (§122) probably proceeded from cases like *jagāma* ~ Goth. *qam*, where *-ā-* for **-o-* was in conformity with phonetic law (§9; older *jagăma* of the 1st sg. can perhaps be traced to a basic form **gᵘegᵘomə̥a*, in which *-o-* did not stand in an open syllable). The Germanic preterites still clearly reflect the stem gradation and accentual alternation of Old Ind.: cf. 3rd sg. Ved. *jujóṣa* "has enjoyed," plur. *jujuṣúḥ* with OHG *kôs* "chose," *kurum* "we chose" < proto-Gmc. **kaus*, formerly **káus-a* (Old Ind. *-jóṣ-*), but **kuzum*, formerly **kusum-é* (Old Ind. *-juṣ-'*).

§124. Roots with medial *-a-* which are reduplicated with their own initial consonant (for example, *pac-*: *papac-*, *sad-*: *sasad-*, but not *gam-*: *jagam-*, *has-*: *jahas-*) form the weak stem without reduplication but with *-e-* instead of *-a-* in the root syllable: *sasad-*: *sed-*, *papac-*: *pec-*, *tatap-*: *tep-*, etc. If the ending *-itha* instead of *-tha* is added to the 2nd sing. act., then this person is also formed from the weak stem.

Paradigm *tap-* "atone for":

Active

	Singular	Dual	Plural
1st	tatapa, tatāpa	tepiva	tepima
2nd	tataptha, tepitha	tepathuḥ	tepa
3rd	tatāpa	tepatuḥ	tepuḥ

Middle

1st	tepe	tepivahe	tepimahe
2nd	tepiṣe	tepāthe	tepidhve
3rd	tepe	tepāte	tepire

The origin of this formation lies in the regular weak forms (e.g. 1st plur. act.): **sa-sd-ima* (> **sazd-*) beside *sasǎda*, **ya-im-ima* beside *yayǎma* (*sad-* "sit," *yam-* "extend"), which must have gone to *sedima*, *yemima* (**az*, **ai* > *e*, §14); the model *sa-sad-/sed-* was then carried over to *ta-tap-/tep-*, *pa-pat-/pet-* (: *pat-* "fall"). Vedic still has *pa-pt-úḥ* beside *petúḥ*, etc.

§125. Roots in *-ā* have *-au* as their ending in the 1st and 3rd sing. active; in the weak forms (and in the 2nd sing. active before *-itha*) the root vowel falls away.

Paradigm *dhā-* "put":

Active

	Singular	Dual	Plural
1st	dadhau	dadhiva	dadhima
2nd	dadhātha, dadhitha	dadhathuḥ	dadha
3rd	dadhau	dadhatuḥ	dadhuḥ

Middle *dadhe*, *dadhiṣe*, etc.

Vedic *paprá̄* beside *papráu* (*prā-* "fill").

§126. The perfect of *bhū-* "be, become" is *babhūva*, *babhūvitha*, *babhūva*, plur. *babhūvima*, *babhūva*, *babhūvuḥ*. For *ji-* "conquer" we have: perf. 3rd sing. act. *ji-gāy-a*, plur. *ji-gy-uḥ*; for *hi-* "throw": *jighāya*, *jighyuḥ*. For *han-* "strike": *jaghāna*, *jaghnuḥ*. *ci-* "gather" forms *cicāya* or *cikāya*.

babhūva is an archaism (: Gr. πε-φυ-ώς), cf. also Ved. *sa-sū-*, §123; the perfects of *ji-*, *hi-*, etc. show that *j*, *h* there are palatalizations of *g*, *gh*, §§18, 27.

ah- "speak" occurs only in the perfect forms *āha*, *āttha*, *āha*, dual 2nd *āhathuḥ*, 3rd *āhatuḥ*, plur. 3rd *āhuḥ*.

A "preterito-present" is *veda* "I know" without reduplication, root *vid-*: sing. 2nd *vettha*, 3rd *veda*, plural *vidma*, *vida*, *viduḥ*.

veda, *vettha*, *vidma* = Greek οἶδα (οἶδε), οἶσθα, ἴδμεν, Goth. *wait*, *waist*, *witum*.

§127. A periphrastic perfect is formed from the derived verbs, especially the causatives, as well as from *ās-* "sit" and from roots which begin with a vowel (except *ă-*) and are long by nature or by position. Its means of formation: *-ām* is added to the present stem of the derived verbs, to the roots of the others, and the perfect of *kṛ-* "do" (§123), *as-* "be" (*āsa*), or *bhū-* "be, become" (§126) is then added; for example:

ās- "sit": *āsām-āsa*, *āsāṁ-cakre*, *āsāṁ-babhūva*;
cint- "think," cl. 10 (*cint-ay-a-ti*): *cintayām-āsa*;
tuṣ-, caus. *toṣayati* "satisfies": *toṣayām-āsa*.

4. Derived Conjugations

§128. The passive is formed by addition of a stem-formation element *-ya-* to the weak form of the root; the endings are those of a middle of the thematic classes (§84).

Cf. *yuj-* "bind": *yuj-ya-te* "he is bound," *dviṣ-* "hate," *dviṣyate*.

Final *-i-*, *-u-* of the root is lengthened before *-ya-*: *ji-* "conquer," *jīyate*; *śru-* "hear," *śrūyate*. Root-final *-ṛ-* appears before *-ya-* as *-ri-*, after a double consonant as *-ar-*; *-ṝ-* appears as *-īr-*, after labials as *-ūr*: *kṛ-* "make," *kriyate*; *smṛ-* "remember," *smaryate*; *tṝ-* "cross over," *tīryate*; *pṝ-* "fill," *pūryate*.

Roots in _-ā-_ usually show _-ī-_: _dā-_ "give," _dīyate_. Cases with an unchanged high-grade root also appear (_jñā-_ "know," _khād-_ "eat," _nind-_ "blame," _gam-_ "go": _jñāyate, khādyate, nindyate, gamyate_). Note also _bandh-_ "bind": _badhyate_, _vac-_ "speak": _ucyate_, _vas-_ "dwell": _uṣyate_, _yaj-_ "sacrifice": _ijyate_, _grah-_ "seize": _gr̥hyate_, _śās-_ "order": _śiṣyate_.

Verbs of class 10 (§83) and causatives (§129) form the passive from the form of the present stem left after _-aya-_ is dropped: _cur-_ 10 "steal" (_cor-aya-ti_), pass. _coryate_; _vad-_ "speak," causative _vādayati_, pass. _vādyate_.

The _-i̯-_present, having become the passive, thus shows, with few exceptions, a zero-grade (§36) root form: _*kr̥-i̯-_ > _*kr-ii̯-_, _*tr̥ə̯-i̯-_, _*pl̥ə̯-i̯-_ > _tīr-y-_, _pūr-y-_ (§13); _*də-_ (zero grade of _dā-_, §37), > _*di-_, but _dī-y-_ with the same lengthening as with _jīy-_, _śrūy-_; also _*g_^{u}_m̥-i̯-_ > _gam-y-_; _*bhn̥dh-i̯-_ (: _bandh-_) > _badh-y-_ (§8), _uc-_, _uṣ-_ (§25), _ij-_ as zero grades of _vac-_, _vas-_, _yaj-_; _*kəs-_ > _śiṣ-_ (§§11, 25), high grade _śās-_.

As future, perfect, and aorist of the passive the corresponding forms of the middle are used, but a 3rd sing. aor. of the passive is formed by addition of _-i_ to the augment-bearing guṇated root, which is usually vr̥ddhied if we have _-a-_ in an open syllable: _budh-_ "awaken": _a-bodh-i_; _śru-_ "hear": _a-śrāv-i_; _kr̥-_ "make": _a-kār-i_; but e.g. _jan-_ "be born," _dam-_ "tame," _ajani_, _adami_.

In Vedic we also find unaugmented forms like _śrā́vi_.

§129. Causatives are formed from the root in the same way as for the 10th present class (§83): _budh-_ "awaken": caus. _bodhayati_ "he awakens," _dr̥ś-_ "see": _darśayati_ "he causes to be seen, shows," _nī-_ "lead": _nāyayati_ "causes to be led," _kr̥-_ "make": _kārayati_ "he causes to be made," but _jan-_ "be born": _janayati_ "he begets." They designate the causing of the action which the basic verb expresses.

A historical explanation appears on p. 72.

Roots ending in *-ā* (*-ai*) usually have as their causative sign *-paya-*, before which *-ā-* sometimes appears as short: *jñā-* "know," *gā(i)-* "sing," *dā-* "give": *jñăpayati, gāpayati, dāpayati* ("causes to be given"). Note *ṛ-* "go," *adhi-i-* "study," *ruh-* "climb": *arpayati, adhyāpayati, ropayati* (beside *rohayati*), etc.

For the perfect of the causatives see §127, for the passive §128; the future is formed from the causative stem, cf. *bodhayiṣyati*: *bodhayati* (*budh-*); the reduplicating aor. (§113) serves as aorist. Participles: §131, 135, infinitive §137, gerunds §139.

§130. Intensives are formed by means of a stem with strengthened reduplication and *-ya-*: *pā-pac-yate* "he cooks repeatedly": *pac-* "cook"; *rorūyate* "he cries very much": *rū-* "cry"; other formations are *vevetti, vevedīti* (: *vid-* "know"), *dari-drā-ti* (: *drā-* "run"), *barībharti* (: *bhṛ-* "bear"), etc.

Desideratives add *-sa-* (*-iṣa-*) to the reduplicated root: *pi-pā-sati* "wishes to drink": *pā-* "drink," *śu-śrū-ṣati* "should like to hear" (: *śru-*). Note *ditsati, dhitsati*: *dā-* "give," *dhā-* "put"; *īpsati*: *āp-* "obtain"; *jighāṁsati*: *han-* "kill," etc.

By means of *-ya-* denominative verbs can be derived from nominal stems, for example: *amitra-yati* "is hostile": *amitra-* "enemy," *dolā-yate* "swings": *dolā-* "swing," *tapas-yati* "castigates himself": *tapas-* "repentance." Note the occasional lengthening of the stem-final sound (e.g. in *kṛṣṇāyati* "colors black," *kavīyant-* "acting like a wise man": *kṛṣṇa-* "black," *kavi-* "wise man"), as well as the occurrence of a stem in *-ī-* for *a*-nouns: *putrī-yati* "desires a son" (*putra-* "son").

The Nonfinite Verb

(*a*) Participles

§131. A present active participle is derived from the present stem by means of the suffix *-ant-*/*-at-*, already discussed in §62: *bhṛ-* 1, *bharant-*; with athematic verbs (e.g. *bhinad-mi*: *bhind-*

anti/*bhid*-) -*ant*- is added to the weak form: *bhind-ant*-. Verbs of class 3 (§§96 ff.) have only -*at*-: *dā*- 3 (*dadāti*), *dadat*-.

Causatives and futures also form their participles in this way: *sādayati* "puts," *bhaviṣyati* "will be": *sādayant*-, *bhaviṣyant*-.

§132. The present middle participle adds -*māna*- (f. -*ā*-) to the present stem in the thematic classes, -*āna*- (f. -*ā*-) in the athematic classes: *bhṛ*- 1, *bharamāṇa*-,[28] *śru*- passive, *śrūyamāṇa*-, *dā*- future (middle): *dā-sya-māna*-; *bhid*- 7, *bhindāna*-; note *ās*- 2 "sit": *āsīna*-.

Cf. -*māna*- with Gr. φερό-μενο-ς, Lat. *alu-mn-us*, etc.

§133. The perfect active participle, whose inflection has already been given in §68, adds -*vas*- to the weak perfect stem (§122): *kṛ*- "make," weak perfect stem *ca-kṛ*- (1st plur. act. *cakṛma*), perf. act. part. *cakṛvas*-. If the weak stem is monosyllabic (*ūc*-: *uvāca*, *tep*-: *tatāpa*, *jajñ*-: *jajāna*, §§121, 124), then the connecting vowel -*i*- usually appears before the suffix: *ūcivas*- "having spoken," *tepivas*- "having castigated himself," *jajñivas*- "having begotten," but *vidvas*- "knowing."

§134. The perfect middle participle adds -*āna*- to the weak perfect stem (§122): *tud*- "push," *tu-tud-āna*-; *kṛ*- "do," *ca-kr-āṇa*- (§20); *tap*- "atone for," *tep-āna*-.

§135. Perfect passive participles (which have active meaning with intransitive verbs) are formed by addition of -*ta*- (f. -*tā*-) or -*na*- (f. -*nā*-) to the weak-grade root.

-*ita*- also occurs beside -*ta*-, usually with seṭ-roots (§37). Cf. *śru*- "hear," p.p.p. *śruta*-; *kṛ*- "do," *kṛta*-; *pat*- "fall," *patita*-. Further -*ta*-participles show peculiarities for whose understanding a knowledge of phonological history is necessary, e.g. *vac*- "speak," *ukta*-; *yaj*- "sacrifice," *iṣṭa*-; *śās*- "order," *śiṣṭa*-; *bandh*- "bind," *baddha*-; *man*- "think," *mata*-; *jan*- "be

[28] -*ṇ*- according to §20.

born," *jāta-*; *dam-* "tame," *dānta-*; *dah-* "burn," *dagdha-*; *guh-* "hide," *gūḍha-*; *lih-* "lick," *līḍha-*; *vah-* "travel," *ūḍha-*; *sthā-* "stand," *sthita-*; *dhā-* "put," *hita-*.

The following sound laws and ablaut laws are to be referred to for the explanation: the zero grade (§36) of Old Ind. *ya*, *va*=*i*, *u*; of *ā*=**ə*>*i* (§11; thus *śiṣ-* is the zero grade of *śās-*, with *-ṣ-* according to §25); of *an*, *am*=**m̥*>*a* (§8), of *an*ⁱ (§37)=**n̥ə̯*>*ā* (§9) [and of *dam*ⁱ*-*: **dm̥ə̯-tó-*>*dān-ta-*, §9?]. Origin of *c* from **k* (§18; *uk-ta-*), of *j* from **ǵ* (and **ǵt*>**kt*>Old Ind. *ṣṭ*, Old Ind. *iṣṭa-*, §§19, 25), of *h* from **gh*, **źh* (§27); **dh-t*, etc.>*ddh* (§30, 1), also **liźh-ta-*> **liźdha-*, *līḍha-* (: *lih-*), **uźh-ta-*>**uźdha-*, *ūḍha-* (*-u-* zero grade of *vah-*); *h* also from **dh* (§27), **dhə-tó-*>*hita-* (*dhā-*).

The *-ta*-participle comes from an IE verbal adjective in *-tó-*; cf. Gr. στατός, Lat. *status*, etc.

Causatives and verbs of the 10th class always form the p.p.p. in *-ita-*; before it they have the form of their stem without *-aya-*: *cur-* 10 "steal," *cor-ita-*; *sthāpayati* "puts," *sthāpita-*.

-na- is rarer: cf. *kr̥-* "scatter," *kīrṇa-* (§20); *pr̥̄-* "fill," *pūrṇa-*; *hā-* "leave," *hīna-*; *kṣi-* "destroy," *ksīṇa-*; *lū-* "cut off," *lūna-*; *bhañj-* "break," *bhagna-*; *sad-* "sit," *sanna-*.

Zero-grade root (**kr̥ə̯-*, **pl̥ə̯-*, **bhn̥g-*); note the lengthening of *kṣi-* and **hi-* (zero grade of *hā-*) before *-na-* (see concerning this M. Leumann, *Indogermanische Forschungen*, Vol. 58 (1942), p. 24) and the assimilation in **sad-na-*>*sanna-*, etc.

Origin from an IE verbal adjective in *-nó-*; cf. Gr. ἁγ-νό-ς, Lat. *plē-nus*, *dignus*, etc.; participial meaning above all in *(*-e*/*o-*)*no-* of Germanic and Slavic, cf. Goth. *bund-an-s* "bound," OCS *nes-en-ъ* "borne."

A perfect active participle can be formed by addition of *-vant-* (§62) to participles in *-ta-* and *-na-*: *ukta-* "spoken" (: *vac-*), *ukta-vant-* "having spoken"; *cint-* cl. 10, *cintita-vant-* "having thought"; *chid-* "split," *chinna-vant-* "having split."

§136. A participle of necessity (also called a future participle or gerundive) is formed by means of the suffixes *-tavya-*, *-anīya-*, and *-ya-* (*-tya-*). *-tavya-* is added to the guṇated root (§35): *kṛ-* "do," *kar-tavya-* "what must be done"; *ji-* "conquer," *jetavya-* "to be conquered"; *bhū-* "become," *bhavitavya-* "what has to happen" (*-i-* with seṭ-roots [§37]); *śru-* "hear," *śrav-aṇīya-* "what is to be heard" (§20); *budh-* "awaken," *bodhya-* "to be awakened." Before *-ya-* vṛddhi and other forms of the root also appear: *sādya-* (*sad-* "sit"), *kārya-* (*kṛ-* "do"), *bhāvya-* and *bhavya-* (*bhū-*), *jeya-* and *jayya-* (*ji-*), *deya-* (*dā-* "give"). *-t-ya-*, with the weak form of the root, also occurs: *itya-* "what must go" (*i-*), *śrutya-* "to be heard, what must be heard" (*śru-*); cf. §139.

(*b*) Infinitive

§137. The infinitive is formed by means of *-tum*, which is added to the high-grade (guṇated) root; frequently, originally with seṭ-roots (§37), *-i-* appears before *-tum*. Cf. *dā-* "give," *dā-tum*; *nī-* "lead," *netum*; *śru-* "hear," *śrotum*; *bhū-* "become," *bhavitum*; *pat-* "fall," *patitum*; *yudh-* "fight," *yoddhum*; *vah-* "travel," *voḍhum*; *sthā-*, causative *sthāpayati*, inf. *sthāpay-i-tum*.

The same sound laws are to be noted in this case as for the addition of the participial suffix *-ta-* to roots ending in a consonant (§135).

Old Ind. *-tum* is originally the acc. sing. of a noun in *-tu-*; the same formation is shown by the Lat. supine, e.g. *da-tum*. Vedic also uses other case forms of *-tu-* as infinitives, such as *-toḥ*, *-tave*, *-tavai*; it still has an abundance of additional infinitive formations, e.g. in *-taye*, *-mane*, *-vane*, *-ase*, *-adhyai*, etc.

(*c*) Gerunds

§138. A characteristic syntactical trait of Sanskrit is its use of gerunds. They are best translated in English by a dependent clause with "when" or "after" (or a participial construction). Cf.: *Damayantī tu tac chrutvā vaco...* "But when Damayantī had heard this speech"; *sṛgālo 'yam iti matvā* "'This is a jackal'—as he so considered..."; *śūnyaṁ vāsagṛhaṁ vilokya* "looking at the empty bedroom..."; etc.

§139. Four suffixes can form gerunds: *-tvā*, *-ya*, *-tya*, and the rare *-am*. Before *-tvā* the verbal root as a rule assumes the same form as before the suffix *-ta-* (§135); cf. *vac-* "speak": *uktvā* (: *ukta-*); *svap-* "sleep": *suptvā*; *gam-* "go": *gatvā*; *sthā-* causative: *sthāpayitvā*.

-ya[29] is added to roots which are compounded with prepositions. Cf. *ā-dā-* "take": *ādāya*; *ni-pat-* "fall down": *nipatya*; *jan-* "be born" and *khan-* "dig" form °*jā-ya*, °*khā-ya* just as they do °*jan-ya*, °*khan-ya*. Compounded roots in a short vowel have *-tya*, cf. *sat-kṛ-* "entertain": *sat-kṛ-tya*, *abhi-dru-* "run towards": *abhi-dru-tya*. Note *ni-han-* "strike down": *ni-ha-tya* (etc.), as well as the double possibility *ā-gam-ya* and *ā-ga-tya* for *ā-gam-* "come near."

°*jā-ya* < **ǵn̥ə-*, §9; °*ha-tya*, °*ga-tya* show *-a-* from **-n̥-*, **-m̥-*, §8. *-t-ya* beside *-ya* is comparable to *-tya-*: *-ya-* with the participle of necessity, §136.

-am: e.g. *kār-am* (*kṛ-* "do"), *vād-am* (*vad-* "say"), *ved-am* (*vid-* "know").

F. Composition

§140. *Verbal Composition.* Old Indic verbs can be compounded with prepositions and thereby modified in their meaning. The most important of these prepositions are:

ā- "hither, unto": cf. *ā-gacchati* "comes to";

abhi- "toward, to, around": cf. *abhi-dravati* "hurries to, sets out";

adhi- "over, to, into": cf. *adhi-gacchati* "finds, comes upon"; *adhi-karoti* "puts over something";

anu- "toward, after, along": *anu-patati* "follows, runs after";

apa- "off, away": *apa-nayati* "leads away";

api- "toward, unto, further": *api-gacchati* "goes unto";

[29] Causatives with a long root syllable drop *-ay-* before *-ya*: *ava-tārayati* "fetches," *avatārya*, but *saṁ-gamayati* "brings together" (with short root syllable): *saṁ-gamay-ya*.

ati- "beyond": *ati-gacchati* "goes past";
ava- "down, off": *ava-rohati* "climbs down";
ni- "down, into": *ni-patati* "falls down";
niṣ- (*nir-*, *niḥ-*) "out": *nir-viśati* "goes out";
parā- "over, through, away": *parā-jayati* "overcomes";
pari- "around": *pari-ṇayati* "leads around";
pra- "forward, forth": *pra-bhavati* "arises, comes to light";
prati- "toward, against, back": *prati-bhāṣate* "replies, answers";
sam- "together": *saṁ-yacchati* "holds together";
upa- "unto, to, toward": *upa-śṛṇoti* "listens to";
ut- "up, away, out": *ud-yacchati* "lifts up, promotes";
vi- "apart": *vi-gacchati* "goes asunder, goes away."

These prepositions are an IE inheritance; cf., for instance, *apa*: ἀπό, *api*: ἐπί, *pari*: περί, *pra*: πρό, *prati*: προτί, *upa*: ὑπό, etc.

Nouns can also be compounded with *kṛ-* 8 "make," *bhū-* 1 "become"; in this case stem-final *-a-*, *-an-* become *-ī-*; *-i-*, *-u-* are lengthened. Cf. *avyaya-* "indeclinable," *avyayī-bhavati* "becomes indeclinable"; *ākula-* "confused," *ākulī-karoti* "confuses"; *śuci-* "pure," *śucī-bhavati* "becomes pure," etc. These two verbs are also compounded with certain adverbs: *alaṁ-karoti* "decorates" (: *alam* "enough"); *āvir-bhavati* "becomes evident" (*āviḥ*).

§141. *Nominal Compounds.* Nominal compounds are very abundant in Sanskrit; with the development of literary style, a larger and larger part of the content of a sentence is expressed by extensive compounds. It can already be seen from an epic text like the Song of Nala that a rather long sentence could, for example, be formed by a dvandva-compound (§142) and a non-finite form, the perf. act. part. (§135) of *dṛś-* "see," in addition to the subject (literally, "[we are] having seen"): *vayaṁ hi deva-gandharvamānuṣoragarākṣasān dṛṣṭavantaḥ* "but we have seen gods, Gandharvas, people, snakes, and Rākṣasas." The ability to decompose compounds correctly is thus a prerequisite for the practical understanding of texts.

The scholars of ancient India gave names to the types of compounds which have come into the terminology of Western linguistics; they are given in the following paragraphs.

In general it is to be noted that the constituents of compounds usually appear in the stem form, with manifold gradation (§58) in the middle or weak form; the "stems" of the pronouns cited in §§73 ff. appear in composition. For *mahānt-* (§62) *mahā-* is found as a first member; final members sometimes change to the *-a*-declension (§39).

For the last two rules the compound from *mahānt-* "great" and *rājan-* "king" is exemplary: *mahā-rāja-* m. "great king." *mahā-* is an older form, to which *-nt-* has been added only secondarily and which still appears separately in Vedic (acc. *mahā́-m*, gen. *mah-áḥ*). Sound laws (§§8–30) and sandhi rules (§33), which also apply in word-interior position, should be referred to for an understanding of the compound forms.

1. Copulative Compounds

dvandva- "pair"

§142. The members of these compounds must be connected with "and" after decomposition, as in Eng. *fourteen* = "four and ten," Gr. νυχθήμερον = "night and day." They occur with dual or plural inflection of the second member but also as collective neuter singulars. Cf.: *putra-pautrāḥ* "sons and grandsons"; *artha-dharmau* "benefit and right"; *brāhmaṇa-kṣatriya-viṭ-śūdrāḥ* "Brahmans, warriors, merchants, and Śūdras." Collective: *sukha-duḥkham* "joy and sorrow." Adjectival: *śukla-kṛṣṇa-* "bright and dark."

2. Determinative Compounds

tatpuruṣa- "his servant"

§143. A case relationship is expressed by the composition; thus in the example *tat-puruṣa-*, chosen to name the type, the stem *tad-* replaces the genitive "his" (Old Ind. *tasya*). Cf. Ger. *Königs-haus* "the king's house." Examples: *videśa-gamana-* n. "going abroad"; *svarga-gati-* f. "trip to heaven"; *aśva-kovida-* "skilled in horses." Sometimes not the stem but an inflected case form appears as the first member: cf. *divas-pati-* m. "lord of heaven" (gen. *divaḥ*).

karmadhāraya-

§144. Karmadhārayas—there is no accurate translation of the Old Ind. technical term—are compounds in which the second member is more closely defined attributively by the first member: cf. *mahā-rāja-* m. "great king" (§141); *priya-sakhī-* f. "dear girl friend"; *su-deva-* "good god"; *su-kṛta-* "well done"; *kanyā-ratna-* n. "pearl of a maiden"; *rāja-ṛṣi-* "royal sage, a sage who is also a king."

dvigu- "consisting of two oxen"

§145. These are determinative compounds whose first member is a cardinal numeral. As a rule they designate a collective relation and usually have the form of the neutr. sing., more rarely that of a feminine in *-ī*: *tri-loka-* n., *tri-lokī-* f. "the community of the three worlds, the three worlds"; *catur-yuga-* n. "the four ages of the world"; *tri-rātra-* n. "space of three nights."

3. Possessive Compounds

bahuvrīhi "possessing much rice"

§146. These primarily adjectival compounds are to be translated by "having [a definite property]," "being in [a certain situation]," like Ger. *Dickkopf* = "having a thick head, whose head is thick," *Langfinger*, Lat. *magn-animus*, Gr. ῥοδο-δάκτυλος, etc. Cf. *divya-rūpa-* "possessing divine form," *mahātman-* "magnanimous, whose soul is great," *an-anta-* "endless, having no end," *su-manas-* "having a good mind, well-disposed," *sa-bhārya-* "having one's spouse with one, accompanied by one's spouse," *prajā-kāma-* "whose desire is offspring, desiring children," *śastra-pāṇi-* "having a sword in one's hand."—*ādi-*, *ādika-*, *ādya-* "first, beginning," more rarely *prabhṛti-* "beginning" as final members express "etc., and the others": *siṁhādayaḥ* "the lions (*siṁha-*), etc., the lions and the other animals"; *ghaṭa-śarāvādika-* n. "pitcher, plate, etc." (= what has "pitcher [*ghaṭa-*] and plate [*śarāva-*] as first"), *siṁha-vyāghra-dvīpi-vṛka-prabhṛtayaḥ* "lions, tigers, panthers, wolves, etc."

4. Adverbial Compounds

avyayībhāva- "indeclinable"

§147. Avyayībhāvas—for the formation of the name see §140 end—are adverbial compounds in the acc. sing. neuter form, with an indeclinable (a preposition, an adverb, etc.) as the first member. Cf. *yathā-kāmam* "according to desire"; *sa-kopam* "with anger, in anger"; *praty-akṣam* "before the eyes, publicly"; *yāvaj-jīvam* "for one's whole life, so long as life lasts."

APPENDIX

Three Old Indic Texts

1. *The Dawn.* A sample of Vedic. (Rig-Veda 6, 64, 3–4)

váhanti sīm aruṇā́so rúśanto gā́vaḥ subhágām urviyā́ prathānā́m /
ápejate śū́ro ásteva śátrūn bā́dhate támo ajiró ná vóḷhā // 3 //
sugótá te supáthā párvateṣv avāté apás tarasi svabhāno /
sā́ na ā́ vaha pṛthuyāmann ṛṣve rayíṁ divo duhitar iṣayádhyai
// 4 //.

"Reddish, bright oxen draw her (the dawn), the darling, who extends far;
she drives away (the darkness) as a brave marksman drives away his enemies;
she drives away the darkness like a swift driver.
Good paths and good roads are yours even in the mountains; with no wind you travel over the waters, you self-lighting one.
You bring us, wide-coursed, high daughter of the sky, wealth as a comfort!"

vah- (§84) "travel, draw" [Lat. *vehere*, Ger. *be-wegen*].—*sīm*, enclit. acc. sg. "her, him" [cf. OHG *sī̆* "she"?].—*aruṇá-* adj. "reddish," Ved. nom. pl. *-ā́saḥ* (§39), in sandhi *-ā́so* (§33, 12).—*rúśant-* adj. "shining, bright," nom. pl. *-aḥ* (§57).—*gó-* m. f. "ox, bull, cow" (§54 [Gr. βοῦς, etc.]).—*su-bhága-*, f. *-ā-* adj. "lovely, charming," orig. bahuvrīhi (§146) "having a good share," from *su-* "good" [=Gr. ὑ-γιής] and *bhága-* "share, luck" [~OCS *bogatъ* "rich"].—*urviyā́* adv. "far" [from *urú-* "wide, broad," cf. Gr. εὐρύς "wide"].—*prathāná-* mid. part. of the root aorist of *prath-* "spread" [cf. *pṛthú-*, see below, =Gr. πλατύς "broad"].

īj- + *ápa* (§§5, 14, 84) "drive away."—*śū́ra-* adj. "heroic, brave" [cf. Gr. κύριος "ruling, lord"]; *-o* according to §33, 12.—*ásteva* for *ástā iva* (§33, 2): *ástar-* m. "marksman" (§52), *iva* "as."—*śátru-*

m. "enemy" [cf. Ger. *Hader*?].—*bādh-* "drive away, expel."—*támas-* n. "darkness" (§§33, 12; 60) [cf. Lat. *temere* "blindly," *tenebrae* "darkness"].—*ajirá-* adj. "quick, active" [from *aj-* "drive on," Lat. *agere*].—*ná* "like."—*vóḷhar-* m., with Ved. *-ḷ-* for *-ḍ-*: *vóḍhar-* "driving, driver" < **vazḍhar-* < **vaźh-tar-* (§§14; 30, 1), from *vah-* "travel."

sugótá for *sugā́ utá* (§33, 2), from *su-gá-* "well passable, good path," *utá* "and" [Gr. ἠ-ύτε "just as"]; *su-pátha-* "well paved, good road" (§66); Ved. nominative pl. n. in *-ā*, §39.—*te* enclit. "to you" [= Gr. τοι], §73.—*párvata-* m. "rock, mountain," loc. pl. *-eṣu* (§33, 4).—*a-vātá-* n. "windlessness" [*a-* "un-," = Lat. *in-*, Gr. ἀ-, Gmc. *un-*, §8; *vā́ta-* m. "wind," cf. Lat. *ventus*].—*ap-*, acc. pl. (§69) "water"; §33, 12.—*tṝ-* (cl. 1, §83) "overcome"; enclisis of the verb.—*svá-bhānu-* (unstressed voc. sg.) "self-lighting," bahuvrīhi (§146) from *svá-* "own" [Lat. *suus*], *bhā́nu-* m. "light."

sā́ dem. pron. "this, that" [= Gr. ἥ, §74]; bound with a verb in the 2nd person, approximately "that which you are."—*naḥ* (sandhi: §33, 12), enclit. pers. pron. of the 1st plur. (§73).—*vah-* with *ā́* "bring to, lead to," 2nd sg. imper.—*pṛthu-yāman-* adj., bahuvrīhi-comp. "with broad (*pṛthú-*, see above) course (*yā́man-*)"; voc. sg.—here and in the following unstressed—in *-an* (§65; sandhi: §33, 10).—*ṛṣvá-*, f. *-ā́-* adj. (§§40, 41) "high, exalted."—*rayí-* m. "wealth, property" (§§11, 1; 56).—*div-áḥ* (§33, 12), gen. sg. of *dyáuḥ* m. f. "sky" (§55); *duhitár-* f. "daughter" [= Hom. Gr. voc. Διὸς θύγατερ].—*iṣ-*, *iṣ-aya-* "be strong," Ved. inf. in *-adhyai* (§137).

2. *Damayantī*. A piece of epic language

Nalopākhyāna 1, 10–12. The beginning of this song has been given above, p. 35. After the introduction of the hero, Nala, begun there, the story turns to the heroine of the short epic and describes how the ardent desire of the Vidarbhan prince Bhīma for children was fulfilled: he became the father of three princes and of a maiden, Damayantī. But Damayantī—

Damayantī tu rūpeṇa tejasā yaśasā śriyā |
saubhāgyena ca lokeṣu yaśaḥ prāpa sumadhyamā || 10 ||
atha tāṁ vayasi prāpte dāsīnām samalaṁkṛtam |
śataṁ śataṁ sakhīnāṁ ca paryupāsacchacīmiva || 11 ||

tatra sma rājate bhaimī sarvābharaṇabhūṣitā /
sakhīmadhye 'navadyāṅgī vidyutsaudāmanī yathā // 12 //.

"But fair-waisted Damayantī obtained fame among people by reason of her beauty, splendor, glory, magnificence, and charm.

Then when she came of age, a hundred adorned maidservants and a hundred girl friends served her like Śacī.

There, indeed, the daughter of Bhīma, clad with every adornment, shines in the midst of her girl friends with a faultless body, like a special kind of lightning flash."

tu "but."—*rūpa-* n. "form, beauty" (§39).—*tejas-* n. "splendor, majesty"; *yaśas-* n. "glory, favorable conduct" (§60).—*śrī-* f. splendor, magnificence" (§51).

saubhāgya- n. "charm, attractiveness" (vṛddhi derivative [§35] of *su-bhaga-*, see above, 1, first line).—*ca* "and" [=Gr. τε, Lat. *-que*].—*loka-* m. sg. and plur. "people, men, world" (§39).—*āp-* +*pra-* "obtain" [cf. Lat. *apīscor, prō*], perf. (§121).—*su-madhyama-*, f. *-ā-*, bahuvrīhi (§146) "with beautiful middle" (*su-* "good," *madhyama-* m. n. "middle of the body, waist"; see below, 6th line).

atha "then, thereupon, further."—*ta-*, dem. pron.: §74.—*vayas-* n. "age, youth"; *prāpta-* "reached," p.p.p. of *āp-* +*pra-* (see above); loc. absol. (§38).—*dāsī-* f. "maidservant, slave girl" (§50).—*kṛ-* + *sam-alam-* "prepare, adorn," p.p.p. °*kṛta-*.

śata- n. "hundred, a hundred" [Gr. ἑ-κατόν, Lat. *centum*, §24].—*sakhī-* f. "girl friend" (§§44, 50).—*ās-* "sit" [Gr. ἧσ-ται] +*pari-upa-* [Gr. περί, ὑπό] "sit around, surround in sitting, serve"; °*āsat* themat. 3rd sg. imperf.—*śacī-* f. (sandhi: §39, 9) name of Indra's wife (§50).—*iva* "as, just as."

tatra "there."—*sma* "truly, certainly."—*rāj-* "shine, sparkle," cl. 1, mid. (§84).—*Bhaimī-* f. (§50), vṛddhi derivative of the name Bhīma-: "the daughter of Bhīma" (=Damayantī).—*sarva-* adj. "whole, every" [Gr. ὅλος], *ābharaṇa-* n. "piece of jewelry, adornment," *bhūṣ-* (p.p.p. °*ita-*) "adorn"; with the karmadhāraya (§144) *sarvābharaṇa-* "every adornment," *bhūṣita-* is joined as a tatpuruṣa (§143) "clad with every adornment."

madhya- n. "middle" [Lat. *medius*]; *sakhī-m*° loc. sg. (§39) "in the midst of girl friends."—*anavadyāṅgī-* f. (sandhi: §33, 5; inflection: §50), bahuvrīhi (§146) from *anavadya-* adj. "faultless" and *aṅga-* n. "member, body."—*vidyut-* f. "lightning flash" (§59).—*saudāmanī-* f. "a special kind of lightning flash, the saudāmanī" (§50).—*yathā* "as, just as."

3. *The One Garlanded in a Grove.* Verses from later courtly literary poetry

Gītagovinda of Jayadeva (12th century A.D.), V, 10–11. The erotic and mystical operetta describes the love of the pastoral god Krishna for Rādhā, the estrangement, longing, and final reconciliation of the two lovers. The following verses are taken from the request of Rādhā's girl friend to Rādhā to give up her jealous reserve and to hasten to the waiting Krishna.

patati patatre vicalati patre śaṅkitabhavadupayānaṁ |
racayati śayanaṁ sacakitanayanaṁ paśyati tava panthānaṁ |
dhīrasamīre yamunātīre vasati vane vanamālī || 10 ||
mukharamadhīraṁ tyaja mañjīraṁ ripumiva kelisulolaṁ |
cala sakhi kuñjaṁ satimirapuñjaṁ śīlaya nīlanicolaṁ |
dhīrasamīre yamunātīre vasati vane vanamālī || 11 ||.

"If a wing flies and a leaf moves here and there, suspecting your coming,
he prepares the couch and observes your path with fearful eye.
Under a quiet wind on the bank of the Yamunā he dwells in the forest wearing a garland of woodland flowers.
Abandon the resounding, unstable ring for the foot, [which is] like a traitor [and] eagerly longing for dalliance.
Hasten, O girl friend, to the bushes filled with darkness; put on a dark-colored cloak.
Under a quiet wind on the bank of the Yamunā he dwells in the forest wearing a garland of woodland flowers."

pat- "fly, soar" [Gr. πέτομαι "fly," Lat. *petō* "seek"], pres. part. (§131) *patant-*; *patatra-* n. "wing, feather" [from *pat-*]; *cal-* + *vi-* "move here and there" [*cal-* with *-l-* (§23) beside *car-* "move," Gr.

πέλομαι "am in motion"], pres. part. *calant-*; *patra-* n. "leaf" [cf. Eng. *feather*]; locative absol. (§38).—*śaṅkita-* "supposing, suspecting, anxious, uneasy" (orig. p.p.p. of *śaṅk-*); *bhavant-* "you," polite address (§62), stem *bhavat-*, before voiced sounds *bhavad*° (§33, 8); *upayāna-* n. "coming near."

rac-, *racayati* "get ready, prepare."—*śayana-* n. "couch, place of rest" [from *śe-te* "lies" ~ Gr. κεῖ-ται, §92].—*sa-cakita-* "fearful; with (*sa-*; see the 2nd strophe) fright (*cakita-*)"; *nayana-* n. "eye"; bahuvrīhi (§146), used adverbially (explaining *paśyati*).—*paśyati*, present (suppletive to *dṛś-* "see") "sees, observes" [full root form *s-paś-*, cf. Lat. *speciō*, Ger. *spähen*].—*tava* "your," gen. sg. of the pers. pronoun of the 2nd person (§73).—*path-*, strong stem *panthān-* m. "way, path": §66.

dhīra- adj. "quiet, slow, continuous"; *samīra-* m. "wind"; karmadhāraya (§144).—*Yamunā-* f. name of a river, Yamunā (today Jumna); *tīra-* n. "bank"; tatpuruṣa (§143).—*vas-* "dwell, stay" [Goth. *wisan* "be," Ger. *Wesen*, *ge-wesen*, Eng. *was*].—*vana-* n. "forest."—*vana-mālin-* adj. "wearing a garland of woodland flowers" (from *vana-* [see the preceding] and *mālā-* f. "garland").

mukhara- adj. "noisy, resounding, talkative."—*adhīra-* adj. "inconstant, unstable" (with *a*-privative added to *dhīra-*; see the preceding strophe).—*tyaj-* "leave," 2nd sg. imper. (§84).—*mañjīra-* m. n. "decoration for the foot, ring for the foot."—*ripu-* "treacherous, m. deceiver, traitor" (§48).—*iva* "like."—*keli-* m. f. "play, dallying"; *su-* "well, very"; *lola-* "unsteady, restless, desiring something."

cal- "hasten, move about" (see the 1st strophe).—*sakhī-* f. "girl friend" (see under 2); voc. sg. (§50).—*kuñja-* m. "bushes, leaves."—*sa-* "with, together with" [IE **sm̥-*, cf. Gr. ἁ-πλοῦς, Lat. *sim-plex*, etc.]; *timira-* "dark"; *puñja-* m. "quantity"; *sa-t*° "filled with darkness, full of darkness."—*śīlayati* "wears, puts on," 2nd sg. imper. (§84).—*nīla-* adj. "dark-colored"; *nicola-* m. "covering, cloak"; karmadhāraya (§144).